Footba

Introducing Polity's new series:
little books that make you THINK.

Quassim Cassam, *Conspiracy Theories*
Stephen Mumford, *Football*
Shannon Sullivan, *White Privilege*

Stephen Mumford

———————

Football

The Philosophy Behind the Game

polity

First published in 2019 by Polity Press

Reprinted 2019

Polity Press
65 Bridge Street
Cambridge CB2 1UR, UK

Polity Press
101 Station Landing
Suite 300
Medford, MA 02155, USA

ISBN-13: 978-1-5095-3531-6
ISBN-13: 978-1-5095-3532-3 (pb)

A catalogue record for this book is available from the British Library.

Library of Congress Cataloging-in-Publication Data

Names: Mumford, Stephen, author.
Title: Football : the philosophy behind the game / Stephen Mumford.
Description: Cambridge, UK ; Medford, MA : Polity Press, 2019. | Includes
   bibliographical references and index.
Identifiers: LCCN 2018043383 (print) | LCCN 2018045663 (ebook) | ISBN
   9781509535330 (Epub) | ISBN 9781509535316 (hardback) | ISBN 9781509535323
   (pbk.)
Subjects: LCSH: Soccer--Philosophy.
Classification: LCC GV943 (ebook) | LCC GV943 .M86 2019 (print) | DDC
   796.334--dc23
LC record available at https://lccn.loc.gov/2018043383

Typeset in 11 on 15 Sabon by
Servis Filmsetting Ltd, Stockport, Cheshire
Printed and bound in Great Britain by TJ International Limited

For further information on Polity, visit our website:
politybooks.com

Contents

1

Introduction

Kick-off

This was my introduction. On 27 September 1980, I paid £1.50 to enter through a rickety-clickety turnstile and then ascend a tower of concrete steps to a black, peeling structure made of corrugated tin, looking to the outside world like a cowshed. There were gaps in the walls, through one of which I followed the expectant crowd. And there it was: a new, magical, vivid tableau stretched out in front of us; a lush expanse of green amid this drab corner of an industrial South Yorkshire city. Thousands of tightly packed fans, adorned in red, white and black, looked down from on high at the same sight. This was my first visit to Bramall Lane, the home to what is now, and will always be, my team, Sheffield United.

Introduction

Everyone will remember their own introduction. The only people I've met who don't are those who were taken first as infants. An introduction is a significant first encounter. Typically one is introduced to live football by someone else, as happened in my case. But it was not the first game I had seen. That was on television: the 1974 FA Cup Final, Liverpool versus Newcastle United. Green, red, black and white: how could that not fascinate a child watching on the family's recently rented colour TV? I loved football right away. Nor was it my first match in person. I'd already visited The Shay, Halifax, and Elland Road, Leeds. But my Bramall Lane introduction was the one that stayed with me as it was a true beginning. Some introductions are by-the-by, quickly forgotten because they fail to initiate anything of note. Others are life changing, and this is certainly what happens when you first visit your home ground. When I ask others about their first such experience, they also volunteer, in dewy-eyed reminiscence, details of who gave them the introduction. A parent, grandparent or friend took them along and an eternal debt is owed. It wouldn't be easy to go alone the first time. Someone has to initiate you into the conventions and routines of how to use a football stadium and how to watch a game. You need to know when and what to cheer and also how to cheer, which I've since found has variation across cultures. Football supporting is a learning experience.

As long as the introduction works, football has you for life. I have never known anyone who stopped liking football. I have met some who have never liked it in the first place, such as my grandfather, who called it 'fool-ball'. But once the love is formed, it is going nowhere. I know some who stopped going to games but they just watch football in a different way, on TV. And there are plenty, such as myself for a time, who get annoyed with creeping commercial interests that corrupt the sport. It wasn't football that I disliked, though, it was what surrounded the game, and I simply went to watch the amateur version instead. Now I've made peace with this transformed version of my first love. I've accepted that I don't stand on uncovered terracing anymore, that the toilets are indoors, that I have to buy advance tickets instead of paying with cash at the gate. I've even come to accept, worst of all, the music that booms out when a goal is scored. In return for my reluctant acceptance of these inconveniences, I now watch a brilliant team. The football is fast and fluid. Sheffield United play short-passing tiki-taka, and commit defenders forward constantly. The players are strong and fit, running tirelessly.

Introduction

They would beat any of the former sides of the past that I knew and loved. This is not only true of my team. All over, we are in a glorious epoch of skill, fitness and tactics. Just consider Portugal and Spain playing out a scintillating 3–3 draw in Russia in the summer of 2018.

The Portugal–Spain game was a World Cup match, which leads me to acknowledge that there are different ways in which we watch football. My preference is always to watch a game in person since I like to be able to look at the whole pitch and see how play and formation develop. I like the fresh air on my face and to be surrounded by others who love football as much as I do. But many watch football on TV, and even I probably still see more games this way than at a stadium. And when we watch on TV, we are usually in a very different position as viewers. At Bramall Lane, I am a supporter, watching in hope of seeing a home win, and encouraging my team to achieve it. In most World Cup matches, I am doing something very different. I typically don't care too much who wins the game, when it is Morocco versus Iran, for instance. I watch because I want to see a good game of football. Of course, that might involve wanting to see some drama and a last-minute winning goal. But I wouldn't care too much whether it was Morocco or Iran who got it, since I am not a supporter of either. So with all the focus we get on fandom in football (see Paul Brown's *Savage Enthusiasm*), and the post-*Fever Pitch* paradigm of watching the game with an allegiance, I think we should not be misled into thinking that the fascination of football belongs only to the loyal supporter. Football has an even stronger grip on us than that. We like to watch it even from the perspective of a neutral spectator, and sometimes even more so, since there is no stress from fear of defeat. There is no supreme moment of joy, either, when one's own side scores a goal. We will come to the significance of that experience in due course.

Infinite possibilities

How can football acquire such a grip on us? What explains its deep fascination? This is what I aim to investigate and I will do so with a philosophical approach. This means that I will be considering my subject matter in the most general and abstract kind of way. But I trust that what I say will make sense to any football enthusiast. Philosophical training is not required, and if this is your introduction to philosophy, have no fear. There are plenty of things that philosophy is not, however. Don't mistake it for the moody obscurantism of José Mourinho, for instance. He may be a brilliant football manager but he's no philosopher. Philosophy aims to make matters clear, not obscure, and being grumpy is not the same as being profound.

Why should philosophy be required here, since football is so simple? Part of the game's success is that it is easy to understand. You just need goals marked at either end of a space and two teams trying to get the ball in the other goal while defending their own. Such simplicity is no doubt part of the attraction. There is more to the explanation of football's universal appeal, however, for the simplicity of football is also deceptive. It can of course be understood superficially but also more deeply, and we can all watch the same game and take different things from it. It is a sport that is easy to grasp. Newcomers can instantly see the point. Yet it also contains a tactical and, I will insist, philosophical richness that will reward attention. There are many facets to football, many levels at which it can be understood. No matter what your level of engagement is, there will be something for you. I will substantiate this claim by defending football's depth. Its superficial appeal I will take largely as given.

Introduction

The multi-layered nature of football, permitting different perspectives and degrees of understanding, is not unique. Football has just 17 laws (not rules, but laws). From these, a vast universe of possibilities is opened. The laws permit any number of possible games. Similarly, chess has just six kinds of piece, each with its simple rules of movement. From them, and an 8 × 8 square board, we get more possible games of chess than there are atoms in the known universe. And we can understand the moves and tactics of chess to any level of sophistication. The possibilities of football are even more expansive, however, since there are no restraints on the number of possible games at all. Unlike chess, the exact same game has never been repeated twice. The same final score of a match re-occurs, of course, but each game is unique in the sense that the goals are scored in different ways, and play unfolds in a manner that no other game in history has ever matched. Different passes are made and the ball's movement follows a unique path each time. There are infinite possibilities open at kick-off time. The spectator is always in a position of uncertainty, and while there might be reasonable expectations as to the likely winner, anything can happen along the way. The understanding of how and why a game develops as it does permits any degree of analysis.

Introduction

Escape

It is little wonder that those who watch football lapse occasionally into thoughtfulness and start analysing what they see on a more philosophical level. Football provides welcome interludes of escape. It allows isolation from the practical and hum-drum concerns of life. These can be forgotten when one is absorbed in a game, enjoying a moment of pure idleness. Football affords the luxury of reflection where one can think about the nature of the sport and what it shows us about life, ethics, the world and metaphysics.

Among such thoughts, one can see how each coach's approach is itself informed by a philosophy: some general over-arching principles or norms concerning what one wants to achieve and how to do so. Perhaps these are articulated only vaguely or in basic platitudes, but they can be powerful nonetheless. 'Win at all costs' sounds a reasonable philosophy to adopt, for example, but we see that it can also be challenged ethically. In *The Republic*, Plato showed the flaw in saying that the good was what was in the interests of the strongest. Similarly, the Argentinian, infamously rough Estudiantes team of the 1960s showed what can go very wrong when a 'win at all costs' philosophy is adopted. The game can become debased and brutalized. Instead, there might be commitments to fair play: playing football 'the right way'. Within that, there could be different views about what is the right way. Does it mean all-out attack? Or are defensive skills among the higher values of the sport? Is it anti football to adopt a safety-first mind-set? Should football allow for the expression of the players' individuality or should they stick rigidly to the coach's system? I say that these are philosophical questions because they are not matters to be settled purely by the facts of the matter. They are normative, concerning what *ought* to be done rather than what *is* done, and consequently are to be settled only through thoughtful reflection. And it is no good saying that one philosophy is better than another because it produces more victories since whether victory is all that matters is itself a normative question. In the case of 'win at all costs', it was rejected as a philosophy despite producing success. Having seen it, most football clubs decided that they just didn't want to win that way. Normativity concerns our preferences for guiding principles, and it's clear that coaches have those. For example, would a coach prefer to win 1–0 or 4–3? This is a philosophical decision and probably one that reflects whether defence or attack is the priority.

Introduction

The coach is at work during a game, of course, and it is his or her livelihood. My experience as a spectator is very different from that of a football professional, however. For me it is leisure time, which allows me an escape from the problems and worries of my regular life. This is where idle thoughts can thrive: idle in the sense outlined by Bertrand Russell in his 1932 essay 'In Praise of Idleness', free from the constraints of practical necessity. Like other sports, football offers the possibility of escape precisely because it is ultimately pointless. Its ends are created and they are not *for* anything else. One farms so that one can have food and builds so as to have a house. But one neither plays nor watches football for anything else. It is for its own sake. Players play to get paid, but this is not what I mean. They are aiming to score goals only because that is the aim of the sport. It is not as if world peace can be achieved or cancer cured by scoring goals, hence what football does is very different from what politics or medicine does, or farming or building. This shows that football has intrinsic value to us. To use the idea of Bernard Suits in *The Grasshopper*, football is exactly the sort of thing that would occupy our time in a utopia, where all our material needs were met. Suppose there was enough food, warmth and safety for everyone on the planet, all of which could be achieved without work. Suppose it was just gifted to us by a generous and accommodating planet. What would we do with ourselves? Suits suggests that we would naturally do the things that are valuable in themselves. We play games, just as we do philosophy, because they are what we want to do: not because they get us something else that we consider valuable, but because they are valuable intrinsically, in themselves.

Here is the explanation of football as escapism: an escape from the mundane, the practical, the urgent, when instead you can enjoy, experience, think and be that child again who approached his or her first game with a sense of wonder. Football is a philosophical laboratory fit for thought experiments. It is exactly the venue for you to consider what is and what ought to be.

Over-intellectualizing

Isn't there a danger, however, that I am over-intellectualizing? Although football can make you think, it doesn't only do that. Indeed, the experience of watching football can be most immediately emotional, visceral, a roller-coaster. Watch the fans in the stadium. Only in occasional moments are they pensive. Most of the time, they are expressive, agitated and excitable. Might one even say that the escape provided by football is that it allows you not to think at all? For a time, you might even forget who you are, such can be your immersion in the game. You are not absorbed in an intellectual reverie, it might be argued; you are watching the football match, and concentrating only on that.

Similarly, for all one might talk about space, time, chance and other metaphysical subjects in football, one might also think it is primarily a game, there to be won with brute strength and individual battles. Consider the vital role of Real Madrid's Sergio Ramos in the 2018 Champions League Final. He had two clashes with Liverpool players, Mohamed Salah and Loris Karius, that seemed to have an important influence over the eventual outcome. Ramos imposed himself on the game in a way that all opposition fans would hate, but anyone would be delighted to have him on their own team. Football is about strength, dominance, subjugation, the humbling, and ultimately the humiliation, of the opponent. Although there are proscribed actions and boundaries which you cannot transgress, within the laws, anything else goes. Football is often dirty and not meant for the theorizing of intellectuals. It is a hard game.

We can recognize and accept much of this, but it does not mean that there is no place for the thoughtful football fan or for a philosophical understanding of the game. Claims that football is a battle of brute strength for dominance and victory are themselves philosophical, presumably made by taking a step back from the experience of any one game in particular and aiming for a general and abstract account. An interpretation of football is being offered and it is one that can itself be considered and, if there are good reasons, rejected.

As a philosophy of football, this hard view should indeed be rejected. While football is to an extent a battle of strength, because strength is one of the athletic excellences of the sport, that is not all that it is, nor is brute strength the only asset of a good football team. Football is conducive to a number of different perspectives and types of understanding because it is, indeed, multi-faceted. There might well be some individual battles of raw power to be fought during a match – for instance, when jostling for position at a corner kick – but this is only one aspect of the game. It also involves speed, skill with the ball for accurate passing and crosses and, not least, tactical intelligence. A successful coach will have a game plan or even a plan for the whole annual campaign.

There are formations to consider, finding ways to neutralize the opponent's best player (such as when Argentina's Lionel Messi was always marked by two Icelandic opponents in their 2018 World Cup game), dead ball routines to invent and practise, exploitation of the perceived weaknesses of the opposition, and so on. It is arguable that the failures of successive England teams after 1966 came not because of any lack of strength but because of these broadly tactical shortcomings. Other countries were thinking the game through better than us while we were still taking a blood-soaked Terry Butcher to epitomize the spirit of English football.

Understanding the passion

We need a balanced approach to understanding football correctly: one that is aware of its many dimensions. Only then can we understand why it so thoroughly engrosses us, which it evidently must, given that it is the world's most popular spectator sport. I do not want to deny that it is a game of passion by prioritizing reason. I aim, rather, to provide a rational explanation of why we can be so passionate about it. The attraction of football ought to be explicable.

Introduction

How do we explain the passions, then? Passion is opposed to action. An action is something that we do, but the original idea of a passion is that it is something done to us: that is, something with respect to which we are passive. Our passions can be roused and we struggle to resist acting upon them. When your team concedes a late goal and loses the game, you cannot help but feel a deep sadness or even anger. You almost certainly don't want to feel sad but are unable to resist the feeling. Similarly, the joy of scoring and winning is just something that happens when your team succeeds. It is not a choice.

There are different types of reasons for why football provokes these passions. There is local and national pride: for instance, when we have teams attached to cities and countries. Sheffield United, in some sense, represents the city of Sheffield; and even though few of its players hail from there, many of its fans do. Though not obligatory, many people support their local team. Pride in, and affinity with, a place can thus be an explanation. But I do not think this is the best sort of explanation, even though it might play a role. While I support Sheffield United, I do not pay much attention to the Sheffield Steelers ice hockey team or the Sheffield members of parliament, who also represent the city. It is something specifically about football that rouses my passions, and this is something that can be thoughtfully considered.

For example, one thing that has struck me as a particular attraction of football is just how supreme can be the moment of goal scoring. This is partly because it is a relatively low-scoring sport. When you get a goal, for all anyone knows, it could be the final goal in the game, even if scored in the first five minutes. It might be the match-winner even then, and this is definitely something to be excited about.

Consider, in contrast, a goal for a side that is already 3–0 down, pulling it back to 3–1. Even with time left, this is not quite as exciting as a goal that could be the decisive one. It offers hope, of course, and could be the turning point of a game, but it is only when the score goes to 3–3 or 3–4 that the supreme ecstasy of a goal is felt. I don't see how a sport such as basketball can ever quite share this, unless it is a rare game-winning basket in the last second. Basketball is such a high-scoring sport that one score near the start of the game can easily pass without raising the pulse at all. Football averages just a few goals per game – some matches have none at all – so almost all goals are important.

It is not just that, however. The rarity of the goal is one thing, but the manner of scoring is also significant. A goal is an uncertainty right up until the fraction of a second at which it is scored. Contrast football with rugby, a sport which I have tried to enjoy but without much success. A rugby ball has to be carried over the try line, and then placed down, to score. As a result, you can either see the scoring moments of a game coming or know that they are not coming. What you cannot get in rugby is a shot 'out of nowhere', from 30 metres, when the defence seemingly had everything under control, but which in less than a second is rippling the back of the net. The swiftness of a goal is limited only by the speed of the ball, which can be kicked very hard, whereas in rugby the swiftness is limited by the speed of a runner. Furthermore, we all know that goal-bound shots can be stopped, sometimes right on the line. The goalkeeper has only a small scoring area to cover so can sometimes make up the ground to save a shot in the last available fraction of a second, on the line. Contrast this again with rugby, in which the scoring area is as wide as the field, so if there is no opponent in the area a try can look inevitable for some time. The effect of a rapidly travelling ball, mixed with the possibility of it being stopped at the last moment, is that the realization of a goal being scored is condensed into an instant. Couple that with the scarcity of goals and you have a very powerful and exciting combination. There is a constant tension for which the rare, unpredictable yet instantaneous release constitutes an overwhelming gratification. Is it any wonder that this provokes the passions?

I am of course making an unfavourable comparison of rugby to football here and rugby fans might point out that I do not properly appreciate or understand the excitement of their game. Perhaps that is true, but I might as well be honest that football is my favourite game and for reasons that I think can be justified, as I aim to show in the rest of the book. At the very least, I think the fact that football is the world's most popular sport is something that ought to permit an explanation.

Thinking to be done

There is thinking to be done, therefore, about the nature of football. And among the things we can think about is why football captivates us so much and produces such intense emotional reactions. My thought about the distinctive nature of goal scoring is, of course, one that any football fan can discern, and I aim to proceed in a similar style. My plan in the following chapters is to consider a number of the distinctive features of football that make it a special game. It has a particular basis and raises some issues that are well worth thinking about, as I will show. My concern will mainly be with our experience of watching football, but not just that. In considering what it is that we see when we watch football, I will inevitably have to consider matters of its fundamental ground. If we want to know what it's all about, we also have to know what it is. I offer little that concerns the playing of and coaching of football, unless thinking about football in an abstract and general kind of way might assist someone in being a better footballer. It would be nice if that were the case but, while I wouldn't rule it out, I am not making such a claim here.

Let it be known, in the interest of full disclosure, that my first visit to Bramall Lane in 1980 witnessed an ignominious 2–1 defeat at the hands of local rivals Rotherham United. But there was still enough for me to take from the game that I wanted to go back for more. The vivid colours of the contrasting shirts against the green background, whose expanse was so much more encompassing than when I had seen football on television, drew my young eye to the fluid and ever-changing action on show as the teams toiled for the two points on offer. Neither fitness nor skill levels were as they are today. Nevertheless, it was one of the most beautiful things I'd seen in my short life, as burly central defenders did their best to negate the 'flair' of the scrawny youngsters who, on account of their underdeveloped physique, could run a little faster than the rest. It was a more experienced player, John Ryan – one of a number seeing out the twilight of their careers at an under-performing but seemingly respectable club – who scored the sole consolation goal for the Blades. But what a moment it was: the veteran bringing all his knowledge of the game to bear in trying his luck from distance, calculating that his best chance of scoring was to close his eyes and boot the ball as hard as he could in full expectation that if the shot was directed just a few centimetres above the goalkeeper's head, that last line of defence would flap his hands around as the ball went by and then jump on the ground when the net bulged so as to show that he was making an effort. To be standing in the middle of the Shoreham End and for the first time to be sharing that beautiful moment of joy and collective release with others all of whom had the same, passionate desire, and were only too will-ing to celebrate together, opened up for me a new world and a new life.

2

Beauty

Football is wonderful to watch. At times, it is capable of beauty. We might as well, then, get the biggest cliché out of the way. Like everything else in football, its origin is disputed, since everyone has heard it and most of us have said it. Football is 'The Beautiful Game'. The relationship between football and beauty is more complicated than the cliché admits, however. Football is also the ugly game. It's the game where Luis Suárez has bitten opponents. It's the game where Austria and West Germany played out an uncontested 1982 World Cup match to eliminate Algeria. It's the game where there are dull 0–0 draws, where there is play-acting and feigning of injuries. It's the game of time-wasting. It's the game of rain-soaked slogs

21

in the mud. Any beauty to be found in football is occasional, at best, and more reasonably should be regarded as rare.

Perhaps rarity is enough, however. It might be worth sitting through several nil-nils to eventually see a 4–3. Ninety minutes of dull and unskilful play could be followed by that one overhead (bicycle) kick that wins a goal in the last minute. The beauty of the latter makes the former a price worth paying. Perhaps there is something to be said for the contrast provided. What makes something beautiful could be precisely that it stands out against the unattractive regular play. The rarity of its occurrence would not undermine football's claim to be beautiful, then. It could be a precondition for it.

Even if it is the exception, therefore, the aesthetics to be found in football could be an explanation of its success. It is pretty trivial to say that we are attracted to beauty. Any such beauty can be analysed and understood, though. What is its basis? How is the sport able to produce beautiful games and beautiful moments? What are the aesthetic values in football? Further, is the production of beauty an aim of football or its purpose? And how do aesthetics relate philosophically to football? Such questions are the topic of this chapter.

Beauty

Behind the cliché

Although we are interested in what it is about football that is beautiful, it is not only the game itself that we must understand. There is also the attitude of the viewer to consider since the aesthetic values of the game have to be perceived as such. Clearly it is possible for people to watch football and experience it in different sorts of ways. One relevant distinction is between partisans and purists. A purist has a wide-ranging interest in the sport and appreciates its excellences. Such a viewer will want both teams to play to their maximum potential and will enjoy any aesthetic value in the game no matter which side produces it (see chapter 2 of my *Watching Sport*). We frequently watch games in this way: for instance, when we are 'neutral', not minding which team wins but just wanting to see a good game. This will usually occur when watching on TV, but you can also visit a stadium as a neutral. The purist contrasts with the partisan. A purist is a supporter whose interest is that their team wins. The partisan backs one side and, in doing so, takes a different attitude to football's aesthetics. For one thing, the partisan would always prefer an ugly win to a beautiful defeat. I cannot think that any exception to this is possible for anyone who remains a partisan. Even a scrappy and dull 1–0 would be preferable to an exciting, end-to-end, 4–5 defeat. Second, while partisans can see and appreciate any beauty created or performed by their own team, they tend not to appreciate, nor even see, beauty created by their opponents. There is no aesthetic enjoyment of the opponent's dramatic late victory, nor even an appreciation of some fabulously skilled action by an opposition player.

For example, I was present when Eric Cantona scored a famous goal for Manchester United against Sheffield United in the FA Cup, chipping the goalkeeper precisely, the ball dropping just under the bar but not so low that the retreating keeper could save it. But I was a Sheffield United supporter and, far from giving me aesthetic pleasure, the goal ruined my night. I might even have hurled shameful abuse at Cantona as he celebrated in front of me. Had I been watching this as a Manchester United supporter, and probably even as a neutral (discounting the fact that neutrality is not often adopted with respect to Manchester United), I am sure I would have seen it as a very beautiful goal. I can also remember how Sheffield United's Brian Deane once scored a similar goal in a league game against Liverpool, and that was certainly a goal I found beautiful.

Beauty

It seems, then, that we are capable of taking an aesthetic perception of some of the phenomena in football or of declining to take such a perception. The distinction between the partisan and purist is not the only way to illustrate this. A gambler who has a bet on the result of a match might have no interest at all in football aesthetics. If he has a bet on a 1–1 score, the last thing he will want to see is a 'beautiful' last-minute winner to make it 2–1. It is unlikely he would see it as beautiful at all. Nor is it a coach's job to appreciate any aesthetics that come out of her team's performance. She wants to see the team win and, in watching it play, is looking entirely at what it is doing, or not, to increase the chances of that happening. If she wants to enjoy beauty, she can visit the art gallery. At work, her job is to deliver favourable results. Of course, she might still prefer a beautiful win to an ugly one, since she wants to please the fans and her employers. But she will share with them a preference for an ugly win over a beautiful defeat. So hard is it to win games of football, I rather think that aesthetic considerations do not enter the equation at all, perhaps with the exception of post-match interviews, when coaches are encouraged into more philosophical reflections.

In suggesting that a viewer has to be in a distinctive kind of position in order to take an aesthetic perception of the sport, I do not, however, want to suggest that beauty is entirely in the eye of the beholder as a purely subjective phenomenon. Mozart's music is beautiful whether someone chooses to listen to it or not, as are Frida Kahlo's paintings, even though there are people who don't understand them. It is still worth considering, then, what the features are of the thing itself that are able to provoke in us a pleasurable aesthetic response. This can be done for football.

Another fallacy would be the view that if aesthetics were an objective matter, then everyone would agree on what is beautiful and what is not. As the empiricist philosopher David Hume argued, however, standards of taste can differ from person to person. This does not mean aesthetic judgements are arbitrary or ungrounded. Some people have poor taste. It is clear that, on the whole, there is a tendency for people to agree on what is beautiful (say, a Van Gogh landscape) if they see it, and what is not beautiful (say, a bucket of sludge). Football adds another dimension to aesthetic appreciation in the case where the partisan declines to take an aesthetic perception of their opponent's works. This is a distinctive feature of the oppositional nature of sport, but it could be compared, for instance, to a rival of Mozart's refusing to enjoy his music or, worse, Nazis refusing to countenance Jewish art.

Given that the beauty of football is not merely subjective, then the way is open for an account of its aesthetic properties, the idea being that there are features of the game itself that are beautiful. What can we say about these aesthetic properties? One thing I want to argue is that they are multi-layered. Some aesthetics are to be found in individual actions, where the human physique and its capabilities are on display, such as when a player performs a Cruyff turn or Zidane's even better version, or Gareth Bale scores with a bicycle kick in a Champions League final. Other aesthetics are to be found in more complicated events, combining a number of different elements. Consider Brazil's fourth goal in the 1970 World Cup Final, which many consider to be the apotheosis of *futebol arte*. It wasn't just the movements of the individual players that we enjoyed. It was the whole combination: the way the ball was passed up from the left side of defence, moved diagonally across the pitch and then laid off by Pelé for Carlos Alberto to run up and smash the ball in. And there is a third level of aesthetics to be uncovered. This is the beauty to be found at a tactical level, concerning position, movement and fluidity of the whole team performance. It takes a trained eye to see this and appreciate the high-level aesthetic properties that the team can produce. Anyone can get a sense of when the team is playing well, though. Even if a team is not winning, you can see when it has cohesion, when the team is playing at a high tempo, when there always seems to be a spare player to receive a pass, and there is always a covering defender for any attack. These are signs of a well-organized and well-functioning team. It might take expert analysis or a coach to explain exactly why a team is playing well, and to understand the subtle tactical arrangements that have produced it, and perhaps only then is the full aesthetic appreciation possible, but it can still be there even to the untrained eye, as when I enjoy Mozart even though I cannot explain exactly what his music is doing and why it sounds pleasant to my ear.

There is a further way in which we can get behind the cliché. The examination of wholes, space, chance and victory will also leave us in a better position to understand the aesthetics of football. In particular, a case will be made for an initially counterintuitive conclusion, namely that it is not in pursuit of aesthetic value that it is produced in football: it is in pursuit of victory. Hence, one cannot produce beauty in football if it is one's primary aim to do so. We will also see that a precondition of the aesthetics of football is the role of empty space, of chance events, and of wholes being more than sums of parts.

Excitement

Just as we considered whether it was possible to take too much of an intellectual attitude towards football, might it also be implausible to suggest that football fans sit and take a detached aesthetic attitude to the game? Isn't there something more obvious about watching football, which is the sheer excitement it can generate? Perhaps it is more the exciting game than the beautiful game. This really should not be denied.

In chapter 1, I offered an explanation for one way in which football is exciting: the infrequency and method of goal scoring makes such moments supremely thrilling. Consider the perfect instance. The ball has to cross the goal line, between the posts and under the crossbar: a relatively small area but not an exceptionally small one, a good size to be seen by spectators and covered by a keeper. It enters the goal, bulging the back of the net. The goal netting was a marvellous invention not simply because it removed some cases of doubt as to whether a goal had been scored but also because of how it made a goal look. The goal nets have been redesigned in recent decades. The rear used to slope from the bar diagonally down to the grass some distance behind the posts, with the effect of killing the ball, making it stationary, after it had been shot in. The move to more box-like nets with vertical backs means that even a slow shot along the ground can jump up spectacularly into the roof of the net. This is not just a practical device: it is designed in such a way as to magnify the splendour of that already crucial moment. Couple that now with a shot from distance, sometimes looping over the keeper, or drilled from outside the penalty area and still rising as it crosses the line, perhaps crashing in off the post or crossbar: the net bulges out, the keeper is prostrate, is there any more exciting moment in a sporting context?

Of course, it is not just the goals that generate excitement, even if they do so to the greatest extent. It is also exciting when a goal is nearly scored, when a swift attacking move threatens a goal, when a penalty is saved, when an opponent is sent off, when a team plays in a fluid, swashbuckling way. Even in the few seconds before the first ball is kicked, the excitement builds as we anticipate the thrills and spills to come.

Yet, can we say that this experience is solely one of excitement? Is the aesthetic experience really separable from the exciting one in these cases? When the ball bulges the net after a long-range shot, might not the intense reaction be because it is such a beautiful and rare moment? It is the greatest and most awe-inspiring sight: one that looks amazing. Watching in a stadium, with a large group of like-minded fans, the experience is intensified. It is a collective experience: a sublime one.

Is excitement, then, an aesthetic category in its own right? If it is, there is no conflict between beauty and excitement, so one would not exclude the other. What else might it be? Is excitement an emotion? It seems not. Certainly it could accompany an emotion, so one could be quietly happy or excitedly happy. The emotion is the happiness. The excitement is something that is caused by the emotion: an effect it has on the happy person, or an expression of their happiness. Similarly in the case of anger, you could be quietly angry or you could allow it to affect your behaviour, manifesting in violent outbursts. Perhaps, then, excitement is a passion, something that happens to us, rather than an emotion, which is an action. It might seem strange to talk of emotions as actions, but one way to see this is to understand that there is a rational structure to emotions, as Ronald de Sousa says in *The Rationality of Emotion*. To be happy that something is the case, you have to be able to see that it is the case and think that if it were not the case, you would wish that it was the case. Similarly, to hope that F, where F is some relevant situation, you must believe that F is not the case but wish that it were. If you could not recognize these things, and understand them this way, you would not be able to experience those emotions. You cannot fear that G if you are incapable of believing that G, for instance. Emotions require thought, and some conceptual understanding, on the part of the holder. Passions are more like feelings that arise uncontrollably without rational explanation. You can certainly be happy to see your team win, which is to have the emotion, but the passion would be the feeling that can accompany that happiness, that makes you jump with joy or scream spontaneously.

There are arts for which excitement is an aim, and this suggests that the passion is aesthetically evaluable. One could praise or criticize a film, a book, a TV drama, a play because it either is, or fails to be, exciting. This shows us that beauty is only one among many aesthetic categories that are at work and available for appreciation, in football or in anything else. A novel, for instance, is rarely described as beautiful. It can be described as gripping, credible, touching, insightful, and so on, but anyone who calls it beautiful is likely to be talking rather casually. Similarly, when we talk of something in football – a goal, a move, a game – as beautiful, it is likely that a better and more detailed analysis of the aesthetics is possible.

Aesthetic categories

Let us, then, consider some of the aesthetics of football and try to produce an initial list of the sorts of things that are appealing to us. We can start with some obvious ones. Speed, power, balance and dexterity are all assets in football, not so much because they are aesthetic properties themselves but because they are productive of something that we do enjoy aesthetically. This is the human form when it exhibits a number of athletic excellences. The body can be fully extended, for example, such as when a player leaps for a header, or a goalkeeper stretches to make a save. Speed helps to win games, but it is also pleasing to watch if there is a graceful, fluid and efficient running style which also gains a game advantage. Strength is an underpinning asset in football, allowing explosive runs, jumps for headers and an ability to retain the ball and repel attempts to be pushed off it. Football is a contact sport, of course, and there are times when it can provide experiences similar to competitive wrestling. When we gaze upon the human athletic form in football, strong, sleek, toned, fast, we can become lost in our experience of the object of perception, forgetting our sense of self. The athletic forms that we see are almost superhuman; indeed, the way we look upon the athletic body has much in common with the way we look at superheroes in comic books, drawn to appear dynamic, elongated and powerful.

Another aesthetic category might hold a key as to why we find this appealing. The category is skill, and the suggestion is that it is pleasurable to watch skills being displayed. It is probably even more pleasurable to be the one exercising the skill, but we can set that aside. To see a footballer capable of receiving a pass from 70 metres and controlling the ball instantly, or playing such a pass accurately, or juggling the ball to escape an opponent, or placing a free kick from distance into the top corner of the goal, can be productive of the same aesthetic experience that concerns us. I cannot be sure why it brings us pleasure to see another exercise their skill, but it evidently does. We like to see people juggle with their hands as well as with their feet, we like to see people who can balance on tightropes, we like to see people lift great weights, play musical instruments, and so on. To explain why this is so will likely take us into realms of metaphysical speculation. We are embodied, rational beings, interested in the extent of human capabilities. Seeing what another person can achieve tells us also what we are capable of, as fellow humans, even if we decide we do not want to develop our abilities to the same extent. I might not be inclined to have the same dedication an elite footballer has, who spends so much time training and perfecting skills. I get to admire what I don't have, but I know what is possible for a fellow human, and, by extension, for me, when I see it.

A higher-level aesthetic category is what we can call simply drama. Football is dramatic, which can of course explain why it is exciting. Drama is an accepted aesthetic quality, of plays and other stories. What might be challenged is whether the action in football qualifies as genuine drama. There are disanalogies. Drama is scripted, of course: the invention of a writer who has a message or moral that they wish to impart. Football follows no script. As we will see in chapter 5, the excitement of football indeed rests on there being no script and the result being genuinely contested. Further, football players are not actors. They can suffer victories and defeats, concussions and broken legs. It is not the characters that the footballers are playing that win or lose; it is the players themselves. When Brutus kills Caesar on the stage, in contrast, no one really dies.

The case can be made for the drama in football being genuine, however, even if it differs from that found at the theatre. Drama can occur in regular life too. A stormy relationship can be dramatic, as can a journey to catch a flight, or a late rescue from financial ruin. Recent politics has also thrown up its share of drama in recent years. Events can be described as dramatic when they involve unexpected twists that are of significance, changes of fortune, just deserts or cruel bad luck. The stage does not have a monopoly on these sorts of events, though it does contrive to depict them. Clearly in football too we get late goals, underdogs beating supposedly better opponents, undeserved defeats, occasional comebacks from two goals down, players scoring against former clubs, incident-packed local derbies, near misses, last-minute relegations and promotions, victories after years of unrewarded endeavour, unexpected managerial sackings, seasons turning from bad to good, triumph in adversity, hubris followed by a loss. The drama is real enough, there for us to follow and enjoy as it unfolds, over the course of a season or within 90 minutes.

Beauty

Regardless of whether that argument is accepted, the alleged disanalogy between football and stage drama can be challenged anyway. Football does follow a kind of script. We know how games will start and end, with the conventional ceremony of a referee's whistle. We know when a game will begin and roughly how long it will last: which is also similar to a play, since its exact end time depends on how long the actors take to deliver the lines and required actions. We know that what happens in the game will more or less abide by the laws of the game, and we know that each team will try to win within those laws. There is a lot that is left unspecified by this minimal script for a game of football, but every script leaves certain things open. This is why any play or film needs a producer and a director, whose jobs it is to interpret the script, in conjunction with the cast. More than that, however, players can be assigned roles by the coach, just as each actor has a role to play. A player might be given the job of ball-winning midfielder, right wing-back, libero or 'false nine', and it will be that player's job to interpret the role. In the next game, that player could be assigned a different role. There is even an oppositional role to be played. Consider Cristiano Ronaldo and Sergio Ramos, teammates for a number of years, but adopting oppositional roles when Portugal faced Spain in the 2018 World Cup in Russia. The actor who plays Caesar need not resent the actor who plays Brutus for his act of murder. Similarly, Ronaldo need not resent Ramos for the foul he suffers, where it is inflicted on him in his role as opponent.

Let us consider one more type of aesthetic in football, which we can describe as broadly geometrical. The geometry of the game seems initially quite simple. As prescribed by the laws, football is to be played on a perfectly rectangular flat pitch, with rectangular goals. It all looks ordered, with precise right angles. But once we introduce two teams and a ball we find that a number of other spaces come into play. There are passes and shots that move in curves and arcs, as do players' runs when they seek to avoid being caught offside. Much is about angles: the angle of the run, the pass or the shot. The defenders and the goalkeepers have a job of narrowing down the angle for the shot, thereby making the goal small. Players weave their way through the opposition, working neat triangles, sometimes launching long balls through the air. We watch super slow-motion replays to fully appreciate this movement within space, seeing the spin on the ball, for instance, that allows it to curl inside the far post. An exemplar was Benjamin Pavard's goal for France in 2018 against Argentina. Is there anything in this sport more wonderful to dwell upon, to contemplate, to be absorbed in?

These are aesthetic categories. But have I said enough about aesthetic value itself? What is it? What is its nature? What makes a category an aesthetic category? The attentive reader may have noted that I have been making certain assumptions along the way that reveal my views on these questions. I think it is right to reject both a purely objective and a purely subjective view of aesthetics. I have no complete theory of beauty to offer but nor do I think that one is required in order to understand the aesthetics of football. What has been implicit in my argument, however, is the idea that aesthetic value resides in a relation between the perceiver and that which is perceived. There are certain features or properties of things that tend to give us – and from which we tend to take – pleasurable experiences. An aesthetic experience is a mutual manifestation between perceiver and object. But I see little hope for a further analysis of why it is that particular features of things are pleasing to us in this way. As with Hume's account, it seems undeniable that humans have shared tendencies to appreciate the same kinds of things. Use of the word 'tendencies' is meant to suggest that this appreciation need not be universal, however. Some people have unusual tastes. But there can be a degree of consensus over the sorts of things that tend to please us. Even if I don't personally like the *Mona Lisa*, for example, I can still recognize that most people do. And there seem to be good empirical grounds to suppose that football has a number of features that a lot of people find pleasing to see. There might be some deeper analysis of what tends to please us. A formalist, for example, might say that the particular things that we like to see in football please us because they exhibit some underlying abstract form. But I would then give the same account of why certain abstract forms are aesthetically valuable: simply that they would be the ones towards which we have an appreciative tendency.

Examples

Having considered in general some aesthetic categories for football, let us now consider concrete instances. I pick two special cases where the aesthetics we have described apply.

First, there is the chip shot. Most shots in football are hit hard, with pace. Accuracy counts, of course, since the shot must be on target. But accuracy without a firm shot is pretty pointless since the goalkeeper will easily get to a ball that is travelling slowly. The chip is the exception. It involves finesse, some say artistry. The chip shot is less often deployed since it is effective only under certain conditions – when the goalkeeper is in an advance position – and it requires a high degree of control and exact placing. Consequently, it could easily go wrong, with a risk of embarrassment for the striker. When executed correctly, the shot involves the relatively slow arcing of the ball over the keeper: slow because it needs to drop down under the bar. The changing trajectory of the shot is something to marvel at, but we also appreciate the shot as a display of skill. The skill comes from mind and body in unison. The striker out-thinks the goalkeeper who has advanced to narrow the angles. The striker must first spot the opportunity, pick the right spot, and then get the exact contact needed. Many such attempts are over-hit and there is aesthetically a world of difference between a chip that goes over the bar and one that falls just under. This shows that aesthetic appreciation does not reside in disinterestedness, as some think. In football, it is because a shot is successful, in scoring or winning the game, that it is enjoyed aesthetically. A variant on the chip is the shot from distance, such as Carli Lloyd's goal from the halfway line in the 2015 World Cup Final. This could only succeed through accurate placement since no shot could retain enough pace from that far. Lloyd saw the opposing goalkeeper off her line and hit the ball over the top. The beauty of such a goal is enhanced by the length of the arc of the ball and the excitement of seeing such a rare event.

The second example is perhaps even more spectacular: the bicycle kick. Here, athleticism and agility are to the fore. It is first of all an ingenious invention (again, its inventor is a matter of dispute), not least because it is also very hard for the keeper to defend against. Because most shots are hard, if the keeper were to wait to see where the ball was going, it would be too late to react if it was not already within reach. So a keeper learns to read the body shape of the striker and from that anticipate the likely destination of the shot. As with the header, though, it is virtually impossible to anticipate where the bicycle kick will go since the body shape of the attacker remains the same, starting with their back to the goal, regardless of the eventual destination of the shot. The direction of the ball is determined by how early or late it is hit: that is, whether the ball is struck straight on or on one side. If it is on target and away from the keeper, then, like the header, it is probably a goal. Its effectiveness is part of its beauty, of course, but if we look just to its beauty, then we should consider the partially circular motion of the feet, ending with one foot as high as it is possible to get it. As an example, look at how high Wayne Rooney rose for his goal against Manchester City in February 2011, with his body entirely off the ground, seemingly suspended in mid-air. Such a shot makes for a stunning photo, but it is still vital to witness the motion too for a full appreciation, and it is even better in a slow-motion replay.

Real beauty is to be found in these examples, but not only in these. All over the field there are numerous displays of skill and athleticism that are attractive to watch. Football has true aesthetic value and that is a good enough reason to love it.

But is football itself art? If we are to take such a question at all seriously, we must answer in the negative. I say this mainly because I think art is a status bestowed upon certain forms of practice by a set of art institutions, and it is clear that they have not bestowed that status on football. If that does not convince you, it might be worth adding also that while the creation of aesthetic value is often a legitimate aim in producing art, it should never be in football. As will be argued in more detail in chapter 6, when you play football, you play for victory, not beauty. That need not, however, preclude the production of beauty in the endeavour to win.

3

Wholes

The team

Football is a distinctly *team* sport. It is teams that win and lose games and trophies. While this is perhaps a most obvious and striking truth about football, it is still frequently ignored. There are sometimes vital players on a team: individuals who make a big difference. Furthermore, in the most immediate sense, it is an individual player who scores a goal. It might be a fabulous goal. It might win the match, get all the headlines and be shown countless times in replay. It is not the team – all 11 players – that puts the ball in the net. It is one individual with a moment of outstanding brilliance: a Pelé, a Maradona, a Zidane, a Cristiano Ronaldo, a Kylian Mbappé.

There are cases where we think one individual made all the difference to a team. Would

Wholes

Argentina have won the 1986 World Cup without Maradona? Probably not. And wouldn't Portugal be a distinctly average side without Cristiano Ronaldo? In cases like this, it seems that one of the players is so much better than all the others that they can elevate the rest of the team with them to glory. The possibility is not hard to grasp. We have noted that football is low scoring. Many games are won with just one goal. In the modern passing game, most of the match is a to-and-fro of possessions, making steady progress in midfield. Chances are few. Even a good team might have only six shots on goal in a game. In those few crucial moments, having a really good player in the key position can make an enormous difference in outcome. Only a very few can remain composed during one of those goal-scoring opportunities. In some instances, it takes a special player to see the possibility of an opportunity: for instance, with a chip over a crowd of defenders. And only a few have the skill to execute certain shots that require precision or power. In short, with such a dearth of chances to score, the individual genius could have a decisive impact on the outcome of a game. Many matches are roughly equal in terms of number of passes completed by each side and percentage of possession. But a brilliant player can turn a game that is otherwise level into a victory with just one moment of creativity.

Nevertheless, I want to defend the counterpoint. This chapter is a defence of the team and also an explanation of why the team is the most important unit to consider in football, rather than the individual player. I will also offer an explanation of why teams can be greater, or worse, than the sum of the talents of the individual team members.

Let us consider the examples again. In 1986, Diego Maradona was undoubtedly the stand-out player of the Argentinian World Cup winning team. He scored great goals against England and Belgium as a result of his individual skill and dribbling. It seems quite credible that Argentina would not have won that World Cup without him. But the rest of the team was also good. They conceded only three goals in the competition on their way to the final. Maradona, with his free role, made relatively little direct contribution to the defence. Nor was he the scorer of the winning goal in the final. Maradona's pass played in Burruchaga in the 85th minute, the latter still having a lot to do to beat the West German goalkeeper, and he did so perfectly under immense pressure (the Germans had just pulled it back from 0–2 down to 2–2). We don't have to deny that Maradona was the best player, and that he delivered when it mattered, but he was only able to do so because he was surrounded by an efficient and well-drilled team. Clearly, had he been on his own he could not have won any game – indeed, no one is even entitled to play an official game of football without a minimum of seven players on the field. Those who were his teammates had to be world-class players. Maradona couldn't defend every attack his team faced, make every tackle that was needed, play in goal, win every individual battle. Argentina faced good opponents through-out the competition, and without a good team they couldn't have come out on top. Now one might say that, even if the rest of his team were pretty good, there was no doubt that Maradona was an outstanding individual. This can be granted, but we also have to note that the Argentine coach Carlos Bilardo allowed him to stand out by organ-izing a team around him. The rest had to provide a disciplined stability so that Maradona could go where he wanted and do what he wanted. Clearly, Maradona should have played a vital role in that team. He was the best at playing the sort of pass that put a striker through on goal and was also best at dribbling through a defence, but he needed support to do these things. A ball winner had to first get the ball that Maradona could dribble, and a crucial pass is only made so if someone else can use it advantageously, as Burruchaga did in the Final.

Let us also consider Cristiano Ronaldo, who between 2016 and 2018 emerged as probably the best player in the world. At Real Madrid, Ronaldo played for an all-star team that had no notable weakness, leading to a string of Champions League victories. But Ronaldo comes from a nation that has not historically been one of the world's most powerful in footballing terms. Only when they had Eusébio on the side, in the 1960s, were Portugal previously a force. With Ronaldo, however, they have become so again, culminating with their first major honour when they were crowned European Champions in 2016. This case might pose more of a challenge to the primacy of the team, since Ronaldo is so outstanding a player. He often seems so much better than any other player in the competition, let alone his teammates, that it is hard not to think of Portugal as a one-man team. Of course, though, this cannot be the case. All the same reasons given above in relation to Maradona apply here. And there is an additional consideration, which is that Portugal-minus-Ronaldo was put to the test and came through it. In the 2016 European Championship Final against France, Ronaldo was injured early in the game, with the score at 0–0. He finally came off in the 25th minute and the team had to play the rest of the game without him, even into 30 minutes of extra time. Nevertheless, Portugal won with a breath-taking long-range goal from Eder. Portugal proved that they were a good all-round team as their defence kept a clean sheet against the competition's hosts. Most importantly of all, the team suffered no adverse reaction to the surprise of Ronaldo's injury and withdrawal. Perhaps they welcomed the opportunity to prove themselves with a positive response. This was in quite a marked contrast to Brazil when they hosted the 2014 World Cup. Having lost one of their best players through injury, Neymar Jr, they came out for their Semi-Final against Germany clutching his shirt, holding it up during the National Anthem, almost as if they were in mourning. They proceeded to suffer the most catastrophic and humiliating defeat in their history, 1–7, as their defence in particular completely fell apart. David Luiz, who held Neymar's shirt during the anthem, had an especially bad game at centre back. It was not that Neymar Jr's presence would have made Brazil clearly a better side than Germany; it was more that Brazil's response to his injury was to lose focus and their nerve and they crumbled at the first setback. It was the team of 11 players on the field that night that lost the game, not the absent injured player. The same 11, in other circumstances, could have been winners; but they lost as a team.

The system and the jigsaw puzzle

This debate, between individual and team strengths, is one that presses upon all successful coaches at one time or another. Any student of the game realizes that coaches need a system – a formation and manner of playing – for these are the matters that tend to produce success. Additionally, it is better if everyone in the squad knows the system and understands how it should operate and how they can contribute to it. If one player is unavailable, through injury or suspension, then someone else can slot into that place within the team. Ideally, a coach finds a system that is successful and it shouldn't matter too much which players are available if everyone in the squad knows what the roles are and how to fill each of them. The coach can, thus, devise the system first and then decide which roles need to be filled. The midfield needs a ball winner, for example, a holder and a distributor. The defence needs a good tackler as well as someone who can win headers from crosses. The attack needs pace but also an aerial threat, and at least one forward should be good at holding the ball up so the others can join the attack. A system also allows fluidity in these roles and movements between the positions. Hence, a 4–4–2 formation can rapidly switch to 4–3–3 when in possession, if one of the midfielders advances, and a 3–5–2 with wing-backs allows players on the left and right who go up and down the whole length of the pitch with both defensive and attacking duties.

Brian Clough was said to be an expert at putting together teams to fit his model. Because his resources were limited, he could not afford to buy star players. When he took over at Nottingham Forest, for example, they were playing in England's second level. He saw the team as a jigsaw puzzle, however. The pieces had to fit together in a certain way, first of all, but he then had to find a player to be each of the pieces. It happened, for example, that there was a piece that was exactly John Robertson-shaped. Robertson was an undistinguished left winger, who was far from a first-team regular and was on the transfer list at the time of Clough's arrival. But Clough had a framework in which there was a need for a player exactly like Robertson. And it worked. The jigsaw puzzle fitted together perfectly, and with a team of players who, like Robertson, had not previously been considered stars, they won promotion to the top division, then won the top division, then won the European Cup (now the Champions League) twice in a row. It was a triumph of the system over individuals.

There are, however, obvious risks with football that is all about the system. Clough did well at Nottingham Forest but only because he managed to find a player for each role. What if you can't get a player with the requisite ability to fill a key role? Or what if you have some very talented players who don't fit into the system? Jonathan Wilson considers this dilemma in *Inverting the Pyramid*, his masterful history of football tactics in relation to the very system-driven approach of the Soviet coaches: 'This was the debate raised by Mikhail Yakushin's preference for the collective over the individualism of a Stanley Matthews taken to its logical extreme. No matter how talented the individual, if they did not function as part of the collective, they had no place within it' (p. 186).

The failures of successive England teams could be attributed to what we might call a system failure. For a period, they had a host of talented midfielders, including Gerrard, Beckham, Scholes and Lampard. But it seemed that they couldn't play together in the same team. If they are clearly the best players at the coach's disposal, there will be a temptation, accompanied by outside pressure, to play them all together. This can lead to attempts to change the system and formation or play players outside their regular position. As England showed, however, this was not a good idea and failed to produce success. The absurdity is obvious. Suppose the best 11 players available are all left-side midfield distributors. That makes a terrible team. You need balance. All the necessary roles have to be covered.

Perhaps, then, Carlos Bilardo found a good compromise in 1986. It looked as if he had 10 players playing a rigid system and one, Maradona, who was allowed to do what he wanted. If that interpretation is correct, it was a system that could support and bring the best out of one exceptional talent. And in practice, other compromises have to be found. It is extremely rare, for instance, that a coach builds a team from scratch. When a new coach comes in, the club owners might make some money available for transfers, but this will usually equate only to a couple of new signings. This coach then has to find a system that the available players can play, with a chance of it being successful. So it is possible to tweak one's system in order to fit the players and work to their strengths. A coach could have a strong view about the best system, but if it's one that the players are incapable of operating, then the ideal might have to be sacrificed to more pragmatic considerations.

Emergence

How can we explain the proper functioning of a team in a way that makes sense of an excellent team being made out of previously undistinguished or average players? Answering this question will also help us to understand how teams relate to the individuals who make them up. This relationship is best understood, I suggest, in terms of the philosophical notions of emergence and holism.

Emergence is a controversial issue in philosophy. Not only is there disagreement on whether there are emergent phenomena, there is also disagreement over what exactly is meant by emergence. This is very problematic since those who believe in emergence and those who don't might have different things in mind. In recent years, however, some progress has been made and we are in a position to offer an account of emergence that seems applicable to football teams.

An emergent phenomenon is one that belongs to a whole and is different from all the properties of the parts of that whole and from the properties that come merely from the addition or aggregation of the parts. Here are some examples. Life emerges from lifeless parts, consciousness emerges from non-conscious parts, free will emerges from non-free parts. Let us take the first example. Each animal is a living thing but it has parts that are not living things. A tibia bone, for instance, is not alive, nor are the many carbon molecules that a body contains. It is the animal – the whole creature – that is the living thing, not its parts, which could not function except as part of the living thing. Being alive is thus a property possessed specifically by the whole. We can say that life is emergent in this sense. It is only found at a certain level of nature: not at the molecular level, for instance.

One might wonder how a property, such as being alive, emerges from parts that are not alive. This question is one for biologists to answer. Some cases of emergence seem very mysterious, however. We have conscious minds and know that their basis is in a network of very many neurons and other components of the brain and other body parts. But those components have no mind: a neuron cannot think. How, then, can many non-thinking parts be added together to make something that does think?

Wholes

When the explanation is given, we can see how emergence has application to football teams. Emergence occurs, according to this explanation, not just when the parts are lumped together. If there is no mind in one neuron, it doesn't seem that there is any in a billion of them either. But for emergence, we need the parts to be interconnected in such a way that they causally interact with and change each other, which is what we believe neurons do. Clearly, living organisms also have parts that are constantly interacting with and changing each other. There's an even simpler example. Water has a power to put out fire but neither of its components has this power. Both hydrogen and oxygen would fuel a fire. So how can this whole have an ability that none of its parts has? Again, the answer is that the hydrogen and oxygen atoms change each other when they enter into a chemical bonding, completing each other's outer shells of electrons.

Now let us apply this analysis to a football team. It's clear that the parts or components are the individual players and the whole is the team. It is just as clear that the parts are interacting. One player's play on the pitch is affected all the time by what their teammates are doing. A player has to cohere with the rest, moving up and down the pitch with them, filling in when a teammate goes out of position, holding an exact line at the back to catch an opponent offside, attacking the near post if another striker attacks the back one, and so on. Offside traps are a good example of this coherence and unity in operation. The defenders must stay in a line: a property they can possess only as a unit. When it goes wrong, such as when England conceded against Panama in 2018, one player gets out of line, deeper than the rest, out on the wing, and the unit is defenceless against an on-rushing striker through the centre. The team captain has a crucial role to play in improving the performances of the other players. They might gee the team up, inspiring them for one last effort at the end, encouraging play with a little more energy, and it is acknowledged that they have organizational duties on the pitch too. But a captain, though important, is still nothing without a team to lead.

There are significant cases where players change each other, for it seems perfectly possible that playing with a team, and being affected by teammates, can make an individual player better, or worse. Let us be positive and focus on the case where an effective team can make an individual player excel too. Very often players are praised for good passes or good crosses. But, of course, they are only good if a teammate gets on the end of them. The second player has to anticipate the pass or cross and be in the right position to meet it. The 'best' cross in the world is no good if there's no teammate there to receive it. We can apply this lesson to a whole team, each player having some kind of interaction with every other one, the team developing a complex web of mutual understandings. In this respect, they are operating as a unit. Only together can they create fine football. Alone, all a player can do is dribble or juggle. If I may add a personal note, my own experience is that playing in a high-quality game has always made me play better, sometimes performing skills I never knew I had, and in one case had never even practised. I am sure many others who have played football have had similar experiences, since I don't believe I am unique.

This account dispels any suspicion towards the notion that there can be teams that are greater than the sums of their parts. There can be great teams that are not made up of great players but players who nevertheless function well as a whole. Nottingham Forest under Brian Clough were perhaps like this. Historically, Germany are an example of an international side that also seems to function perfectly as a team even though they apparently do not have the best players. This comment should be qualified, of course. Given that football is about winning, and is a team sport, perhaps this should make us reassess what we take a great player to be. It is not necessarily one with lots of flair and 'individuality', perhaps as Wayne Rooney was in his heyday. Rooney won no honours at international level. Instead we could think of a great player as one who can function within and contribute towards a great team. In the German side that beat Brazil 7–1, there was a group of players who knew their roles within the system and could operate as a whole. Their football was so fluid and scintillating that it looked effortless at times, almost as if they had a single collective mind between them. In particular, the fourth and fifth goals that they scored in that game looked as if there was a telepathic understanding between the players. How else could one explain the swiftness of the passes and the anticipation of the movements of teammates? The German team was a single, organic entity that night. Rightly, they became champions, and the players did not need fancy step-overs or trick shots to be supreme.

The opposite case is clearly possible, of course, where a badly constructed team fails. There might be good players who bring out the worst in each other and the whole is considerably less than the sum of the parts. It is also possible that those who seem like poor players in a bad team could eventually become good players in a good team. One job of a club scout is to spot players in the lower leagues who could be a cheap transfer but of whom it is suspected that they could do a good job in a much better side.

Opposition

There is one factor which is highly relevant to this but which I have barely even mentioned yet. As well as being a team sport, football is an oppositional sport. Of course, all competitive sports are against others, but by oppositional I mean something specific. In some sports, the competitors take turns, as in darts, golf and bobsleigh. While one player or team has their turn, the other has to wait and can do nothing other than prepare. Significantly, there is nothing that one opponent can do within the rules of the game to stop or interfere with the turn of the other opponent. Thus, in golf, one player cannot push another just as their putter is about to strike the ball, and in bobsleigh, one team cannot barge the other's sleigh as they are on their way down. By oppositional, I mean a sport where both sides are trying to play to the best of their ability while at the same time trying to stop the other team from doing so. Hence, it is all well and good having a plan to win the game, but the problem is that there is another team in the way. Opponents will have their own plan that you must try to stop. We also see that in some sports the teams have their turns simultaneously, but it is still not oppositional in my sense, such as in rowing, where the crews all set off together but are not allowed legally to interfere with each other's efforts. The only legal and acceptable interference I can think of for non-oppositional sports is psychological, where you can put mental pressure on an opponent by a relentlessly excellent performance. If one crew sees the other row away powerfully into the lead, it might discourage them. Or if one darts player seems unfailingly to throw 180s each turn, the opponent could crumble.

This chapter has developed a defence of holism about teams, taking them as single entities and, when they are functioning well, performing like individual organic units in their own right, almost as if the team possesses a collective mind. The fact that football is oppositional adds a further complication to this. A team does not merely interact within itself, with team members affecting how each other plays; a team has no choice but to interact with the opposing team too. Football might be understood as all about this interaction. A player has the task of not just playing well but also stopping their opponents from playing well, by outrunning, outjumping, out-passing and out-scoring them. It's great if Sheffield United score four, but not if Fulham score five in return. A football match is like the story of the two men and the bear. Neither man can outrun the bear but they each need only outrun the other. Similarly, a forward run might be enough to latch on to a long ball against one defender but not against another. A good performance then becomes a relative matter.

With the account of teams as wholes, we are justified in the attributions we make to teams. We say that the team has played well or badly, that the team won, lost or drew, that it is low on confidence, and so on. These things can be true even when they are not true of the individual players within the team. Luka Modrić might not have won the game in which he played, even though his Croatia team did. The oppositional aspect of football takes this idea up a level in that we have to consider the whole game as a complex, adversarial interaction between two teams. Another aspect of this interaction will be considered in the next chapter.

4

Space

Spatial awareness

In watching a game of football, our attention is
often taken by individual players, especially those in
possession of the ball, and the tackles, encounters,
shots saved or successful, the actions of the referee,
and so on. Television coverage usually focuses on
these kinds of incidents, almost always following
the ball. But there is something equally important
that is easy for the casual spectator to overlook.
Football is just as much about empty space, where
the ball isn't, as it is about the places on the field
that are filled with action. To understand football,
and what leads to success in the game, you need
to understand space. The key attribute is spatial
awareness, though this can mean a lot of different
things.

Space

Very obviously, football is played within a space, even if it is vaguely delineated. This space is not simply the playing field. The pitch is marked out by lines, giving it an extension in two dimensions, length and breadth. But the boundaries have a degree of vagueness in that while the ball must not go beyond the touchlines, the players can. Momentum often carries players outside on to what we are starting to call the 'apron' of the pitch, and it is perfectly legitimate for a player to run along just over the touchline, dribbling the ball, as long as it does not completely cross that line. As space becomes limited, it is quite normal for much of the action to take place on or around this boundary. In the design of new stadiums, this apron area is getting bigger and bigger. One might compare its extent at the new Wembley, for example, with that of an old-fashioned ground, such as Rochdale's Spotland. As the game gets faster and more powerful, players need a larger area out of touch.

What about the space of football's third dimension? Neither the ball nor the players are confined to movements in the first two dimensions, since not all passes and shots are completely along the grass. Crosses and shots are usually off the ground, hence height comes into the equation. The header is a vital part of the game precisely because it has this third dimension. Unlike the first two, however, this has no theoretical limit (except for those games that occur at indoor stadiums, with a roof). While the crossbar has a specific height, and there is thus a height limit for a shot to be on target, in theory the space in which a game occurs is of infinite height. In practice, however, there are, of course, limits to how high players can jump and balls can be kicked.

Football is played within a fourth dimension, too: namely within a temporal space. In almost all games, this is 90 minutes in two equal halves plus additional stoppage time at the referee's discretion. In some amateur games this duration is shortened, while in some games there is a necessity of 30 minutes of extra time. When a game kicks off, or extra time kicks off, players and spectators understand that this temporal space is of a known duration and now even the referee's additional time is announced at its commencement. There was a period when this was not so, however. In the 1990s the 'golden goal' was introduced for games in extra time. This meant that no one knew how long the match would last since it was stopped the instant a team scored. It is notable that this experiment did not last, probably for the broadly aesthetic reason that it felt unsatisfactory when a game was halted suddenly with the other side having no chance of reply.

Space

Contested space

Football is about space in a more interesting and fundamental sense, however. Because it takes place within a bounded area, in practice football becomes a contest for the exploitation, control and dominance of space. Just think of all the things we say when we are talking about space in football and consider how metaphorical or literal we are being. We exploit space, we leave space, space is attacked or – defensively – space is covered, watched and marked. It is a failure when space is left because a defender's job is to close down space. An attacker's or midfielder's job is to find it. German international Thomas Müller is known as the *Raumdeuter*: the space interpreter. Possibly more than any other game, empty space is the thing most sought. It is the key to victory.

Space is contested because of what it gives you. Space creates the match-winning opportunity. A midfielder wants empty space to dribble into. The most effective pass is not to feet but to an empty space in front of an attacker, onto which they can run. A striker needs space in which to get their shot away. A free header is one where there is no opponent near to you as you rise. If you get one in the penalty area, you are expected to score.

Space

Space determines the possibilities. If you have space, you can do things that you cannot do without it. If you have space, you have time, since spacetime is a single thing in physical theory. If no defender is near the striker, they are able to steady themselves, pick their spot, and execute it before any opponent can attempt a tackle or block. Since space is such a valuable commodity in the game, hard fought and won, the best strikers are those who can be effective with only a little of it. Only 'half a yard' might be needed by the very best.

Is it any wonder, then, that various systems of tactics have been developed primarily to create exploitable space? This seems the best explanation of changes in formations and styles, for example. Yet, with the increasing fitness and strength of players, such space has become harder and harder to find, making it even more precious. Again, tactics have to evolve and find cleverer ways of creating space.

Compressed space

Most football fans will have seen *catenaccio*, or some variant of it, being played. The simplest way to understand this tactic is that it depends on conceding possession and defending deep. It can be extremely frustrating when it is played against your own team, especially when it is successful. It requires a well-organized defence and also fast and effective strikers. I used to hate seeing teams prosper using this approach. It was mainly an Italian invention, often credited to Nereo Rocco in the 1950s, but used most effectively by Internazionale under Alfredo Foni and then Helenio Herrera in the late 1960s and early 1970s. It seems unjust when one side dominates possession and still loses. It also looks as though one team is making all the running, trying to be adventurous and positive, seeking to win the game, and they then end up losing to negative tactics.

I've come to think, however, that this judgement is superficial. When you see football as a contest for control of space, *catenaccio* suddenly makes perfect sense as an effective and rational way to play. If you use it, your opponents find there is no space at all in your end of the pitch. If the penalty area is crowded, there's no free space for a striker to attack and any hopeful cross will be headed clear by a defender. Opponents will be left pointlessly passing the ball from side to side, looking for non-existent openings. However, if the defence do manage to get the ball, a quick long pass can find vast swathes of empty space in the opposing half. Just two or three forwards joining an attack means that they will be able to run or dribble where they please, with few opponents present, and they will find far better goal-scoring opportunities than they have allowed at their own end. It follows from this that possession statistics, which are now regularly given, are fairly meaningless. It might even be that a low percentage of possession increases your chance of success, especially if your defence is solid and you have some fast strikers. Consider Leicester City's surprise Premier League success of 2015–16, which was achieved with an average of 37% possession in their games. A typical match near the end of the season was away at Sunderland. Leicester won 2–0 and both goals came when the ball was turned over and immediately played long for Jamie Vardy, who had the pace to exploit the empty space and the coolness to beat the goalkeeper. These were both moves of one pass out of Leicester's own crowded half. There are other innovations that can have a similar effect of closing down space. It is not just a matter of packing the defence. One innovation is the sweeper or libero who plays behind the main defenders. An attacker might beat a defender but then finds that the usual empty space behind is patrolled by an extra player, and it is very hard to beat both in one move.

Space

It is common to think of a player as finding space, attacking it or closing it down, but in Wilson's *Inverting the Pyramid*, we also hear more metaphysically abstruse ideas such as 'controlling space' (p. 366, from Arrigo Sacchi) and 'compression and manipulation of space' (p. 339, from Ciro Blažević). The aim should be to minimize the space when the opponents are in possession and maximize the space when you are in possession. The Dutch side of the early 1970s under Rinus Michels was expert at this. Although Michels was associated with the philosophy of Total Football, in which every player could play in every position such that they were able to be anywhere on the field that was needed, there was a simpler tactic which was just as effective. The Dutch played a high line in defence, keeping their opponents pinned back, while simultaneously playing a pressing game so that no opponent had the space to find a killer pass through the orange lines. This meant that their opponents could do little with the ball, and when the Dutch won it back, they did so in dangerous areas.

Giving no time on the ball equates to giving no space away. Other managers, such as Sacchi, had success playing what Marcelo Bielsa called a 'short team', with play being compressed into a central area as little as 25 yards from front to back. The trend has been towards more 'diminution of space' (Wilson, p. 181) through these tactical changes coupled with increasing speed and fitness. Teams aim to 'strangle the space' of their opponents. Perhaps the most extreme case of this is 'parking the bus', notoriously deployed with success by José Mourinho's Chelsea in a 2014 win at Liverpool. The metaphor suggests defending so deep and in such numbers that it is almost as if a bus is parked sideways up against the goal and there is no longer any space at all through which even the ball could pass into the net.

Instability and flux (and Hegel!)

The battle to control space has resulted in a succession of tactical changes, a very obvious case being the changes to formations. Some formations have come to dominate, as the W–M did for many years: five forwards arranged as the points of a W and five defenders arranged as the points of an M. In numbers, the W–M could be seen as a 3–2–2–3. This held sway over a long period as it seemed the optimal way to cover all the important parts of the field. As happens in football from time to time, however, a change can be tried that proves effective against a standard formation. Brazil played a 4–3–3 to win the 1958 World Cup, with Mario Zagallo given freedom to advance on the left side when Brazil had the ball, converting rapidly to what was effectively a 4–2–4. Now it seemed as if Brazil had four against three in both defence and attack, with the midfield not suffering due to Zagallo's mobility. Various ways were found to exploit the weakness of W–M, choking the space for its attackers and dominating the space of its defenders. Subsequent changes have seen 4–4–2 having a long period in the ascendancy, followed by 4–5–1, midfielders forming a diamond in the centre. Currently, 3–5–2 is in vogue, played by England in their 2018 World Cup, encouraged by its noteworthy success for two years at Sheffield United.

We can interpret these changes as further attempts to exploit and control space, seizing upon the gaps left by opponents' formations. It might be wondered whether there is an optimum, perfect formation, and perhaps this is what a coach dreams about at night: the magical line-up that will beat any other. There is an obvious flaw in such an idea, however. If a new kind of formation is adopted and it proves successful, it attracts attention. Football matches are open to the public and television cameras record everything, from multiple angles. There is no hiding place for a successful innovation and, pretty quickly, it will be found out. Consequently, either a successful distribution of players over the playing space will be copied by other teams or a way will be found to neutralize it. Change will become the norm, therefore. Indeed, any team or coach who stands still, and does not look for further innovation, will fail. Successful coaches are often lured to bigger clubs in the hope that they can reproduce their success. What made a coach successful five years ago has no guarantee of working now, though. And if a coach only understands and wants to play one way, they will likely flop.

Football tactics can thus be understood as following a Hegelian structure. Philosopher G. W. F. Hegel proposed that progress in history was driven by a rational 'dialectical' process in which a thesis is countered by an antithesis before a synthesis emerges that accepts what is good in each of the thesis and synthesis and rejects what is of no use. This seems applicable to football tactics. Some thesis is proposed: a new system or style of play that produces success. Other teams have to respond to it and make changes in their own style of play. They seek to provide the antithesis that neutralizes the existing style. From these two we settle on a synthesis, taking the best of both competing systems. The synthesis might reign for a while, but it effectively constitutes a new thesis, which coaches will be trying to counter. Tactics evolve, therefore, motivated by the overriding goal of success. Formations get found out, neutralized and changed. This is how football develops.

Two pre-Socratic philosophers gave us opposite views of the world. Parmenides said that change was impossible, including motion, since that was a change in position. The antithesis to that was provided by Heraclitus, who said that everything was in motion constantly. The world was always in flux. The Parmenidean position may have had philosophical arguments on its side, but it had no confirmation in experience. We see changes all the time. Football needs a Heraclitean interpretation. In football matches, immediately, but also when one looks at the evolution in football tactics, we find a Heraclitean flux in which there is ceaseless movement, battling for space.

Football is the opposite of motionless in a very obvious sense. Players, and the ball, have to move constantly. When we look at formations, we should not think of them as indicative of fixed positions where the players stand. At best, the representations of formations show us relative areas in which the players move, sometimes operating as a unit, as a defence must do for offside purposes. Mostly, however, football requires mobility and fluidity, often with rotation of positions. These are essentially spatial matters, since movement can only occur within a space. Successful footballing philosophies will thus have to adopt at least some stance towards space and movement.

Goals and the unoccupied place

Empty space has to be understood in terms of absence, since an empty space in football is a place where there is no one present. This might seem like an unnecessarily obscure and metaphysical way of describing such a simple game as football but we can see that emptiness and absence take us to the heart of the matter, including of the most vital part of the game, goal scoring. As I said above, a striker needs space in which to score. The best strikers don't need much of it – that's what makes them the best – but they still need some.

Gary Lineker once explained some of his goal-scoring success in these terms. When he judged that a ball was about to be played into the penalty area, he would look for and 'attack' an empty space: where the defenders were absent. The priority was to lose his marker rather than know the ball was coming to him. Indeed, when a ball is played into the danger area at speed, if you are not already in the rough vicinity of its destination, then you have little chance of getting to it. It is pointless, in most cases, to watch the crosser of the ball if it is whipped in, since by the time it leaves their foot, it is already too late. (There are, of course, exceptions, such as if the ball is hung up in the air, or if you are the only attacker in the area, in which case the ball might be played deliberately to you.) The Lineker solution, then, was to lose his marker and go to the empty space just a few moments before the cross was launched. In most cases, his run came to nothing as the ball didn't reach him. But he was playing the odds. He knew that on some occasions he would get lucky and the ball would come his way. Given that he was then in empty space, he would have the time to get away a decent attempt on goal. The statistics prove the efficacy of his approach. Look for absences. Look for where the defenders are not.

If you want a perfect demonstration of this philosophy, consider Thomas Müller's opening goal in that 2014 World Cup Semi-Final against Brazil. It came from a corner kick aimed roughly at the space between the six-yard line and the penalty spot. Defenders and attackers jostled for position, moving around and looking for space before the kick was even taken. While three German attackers moved to the near post, Müller dropped further back, away from everyone else, and he got lucky. The corner came just right for him. He had so much empty space that he was able to simply side-foot the ball home from seven yards. He didn't even need to win a header due to the absence of any defender. The ball was in the air for less than a second and he had so much space that no defender had a hope of reaching him and challenging for the ball. Of course, the defence failed badly on this occasion. Someone should have followed Müller when he went into the vacant space. But the Brazilians might also have been played. Notice how those three German attackers, in moving to the near post, took almost the whole of the Brazilian defence with them. Did the Germans fool the defence with a pre-arranged routine, designed to create a pocket of empty space right in front of goal? It seems possible and, in the game, it was the breakthrough strike that opened the floodgates.

An absence is where something isn't, and there are different absences, some of which can be in the same place. A striker might see that the space around the penalty spot is unoccupied, meaning that they see an absence of every other player there.

Space

Absences are peculiar things, though, because the penalty spot also has an absence of an elephant and the absence of Freddie Mercury. These latter two absences are irrelevant, though, and we seem able to discern the relevant absences of an empty space. The penalty spot is a place where there could plausibly, in normal circumstances, be a defender, which is what the striker knows to look for. There could be contexts in which one sees an absent elephant there instead, such as if a herd of elephants has escaped near the stadium and everyone is assisting rounding them up. But in the context of a football match, empty spaces mean places in which other players are not.

It might seem that I am labouring this point, but on reflection we see that such empty spaces play an even more vital role in goal scoring. It is not just that the striker needs to find space in which to shoot, but that the ball's actual crossing of the line depends essentially on it too. When a striker places a shot, they are looking for a place between the posts and under the bar where the goalkeeper or a defender is not. Every goal depends upon the absence of someone in the place where the ball goes, since had the goalkeeper been there, the shot could have been stopped. One sort of goal that is particularly pleasing to see is a shot or header back across goal where, when it was made, it was directed at the goalkeeper; but the keeper is already moving away and by the time the ball reaches the line, the space is no longer occupied.

One can generalize such an understanding of goal scoring to football in general. Just as a goal depends on the absence of anyone who could stop it, all successful acts in the game depend on similar absences. A cross is a good one because of the absence of anyone who blocks it; a run is possible only because of the absence of someone in the way; a pass is poor because of the absence of anyone receiving it. More crucially, three goals win the game only because the opposition didn't score four. What is, then, seems also partly constituted by what isn't, and glory rests upon the exploitation of these little patches of absence.

This idea might make more sense to defenders. Midfielders and attackers have to be creative since their job is to make things happen. If you are playing defensively, however, your job is the opposite. You are trying to stop things happening, namely goals and serious chances of goals. An attacker has a good game if things happen; a defender has a good game if nothing happens. The defence wants a clean sheet, and with good reason. One of the many beauties of football is that a good defence is just as important for success as a good attack since the win depends not just on how many you score. The aim is to concede fewer.

Space and place

Football exhibits flux inside its space. But we need not accept that there is no fixed place within this space. Places are important too. Positions might be occupied only fleetingly, but they are still there and significant. Not every place on the field is unoccupied during the game, of course. Each player always has a position, even if it constantly changes. Everyone has to be somewhere, and that counts when you look to play a pass or are seeking to penetrate a massed defence. The empty spaces, too, have a position.

When I say that places on a football pitch are significant, I am thinking of the areas and locations that seem to have special powers. Take the penalty area. A defensive foul committed here leads to a penalty kick and a high chance of a goal. The penalty spot itself has a particular significance since it is the scene of so much excitement, heartbreak and joy, not least at a penalty shoot-out. The centre circle excludes opponents at kick-off. The half-way line marks a boundary at which the offside rule applies, since no one can be offside in their own half. The corner quadrants mark a limit for the placement of balls at corners. The penalty arc excludes defenders at penalty kicks, allowing the taker an unimpeded run-up. Places count, and they count tactically too. Marcelo Bielsa emphasized winning the ball 'high up the field'. It is more valuable to do so there than deeper into one's own territory since the latter presents a risk of conceding, the former a chance of scoring.

The most special place of all is the goal and its vicinity. Immediately in front, the 'face' of the goal, is the area of greatest crisis or opportunity, depending on your perspective. The defence protects it at all costs, sometimes employing a zonal marking system. In the extreme case, witness those occasions on which an indirect free kick is awarded in the penalty area and the whole defensive team occupies the line. See, too, the lengths to which any defensive player or keeper will go: throwing 'their body on the line' in order to keep out the ball. Though it is not strictly within the field of play, the space within the goal, between the line, posts and netting, becomes the most precious location on the whole field. It's the sacred place the attack wants to penetrate; it's the place regarded as a home base for the defence, even though it is but another empty space.

Space

Except for the usual goalkeeper's towel, spare gloves and water bottle, one would think there is very little worth protecting in this enclosure, yet in the game situation it is everything. Many fans gather right behind the goal, even though such a vantage point provides a terrible view of the rest of the match. For some, it is worth the risk of missing almost everything else in return for the closest view of the ball hitting the net; and before the days of all-seater stadiums, it was common for fans to change ends at half time to be always close to the action that counts.

Football pitches are themselves located in a space. The stadium contains a pitch but is much more than that, including the stands, the walkways, the turnstiles and exterior walls, towards which supporters feel an attachment. I confess to a feeling that Bramall Lane, my own stadium, has a boundary that creeps out beyond its own confines. When I walk along Shoreham Street, Baron Street or Bramall Lane itself, I am already in a special place. The thrills have already begun. I've sometimes been passing by when there was not a match on and still felt excited. It is not just that there is an advantage for Sheffield United when it plays at Bramall Lane. It is demonstrable statistically that the away side tends to do worse. Primarily, the place is special for the team and fans because it is a home from home.

5

Chance

The ball is round

Anything can happen in football. No one ever knows the result in advance as long as it is a fair game. There might very occasionally be some fixed games, but these seem the only cases where the score is pre-determined. In all other matches, the win is up for grabs. Even when the weakest team in a competition plays the strongest, we know that they still have a chance. This is sometimes considered the beauty of football. It can deliver surprises. The German coach Sepp Herberger said, 'The ball is round, the game lasts 90 minutes ... everything else is pure theory.' Only a pedant would point out that, technically, the ball is spherical, since 'round' is more poetic here. Nor is this merely a claim about the shape of the ball, since the bounce of a round ball is easier to predict than that of an egg-shaped rugby ball. Herberger was saying that all we know in advance is the shape of the ball and the length of the game. After that, no one can predict anything with certainty since anything can happen.

Why, though, think that unpredictability is desirable? One thing it means is that everyone has a chance. When the game kicks off, players and fans alike know that, no matter the circumstance, regardless of how out of form or in form their team might be, irrespective of how many star players are lining up against you, the result is still there to be fought over. Of course, a very weak side will have only a small chance of winning against a very strong side. But a small chance is still a chance. Crucially, the result depends only on what happens over the 90 minutes. Past records count for nothing. Unless a team performs well during that match, it can lose.

There have been some great shock results in football, and these undoubtedly are part of the sport's attraction. These historical results become part of the game's mythos because they demonstrate that the unpredictability of the game is a fact. They act as a warning against complacency to any team taking its success for granted. From the other side, historical shocks serve as an inspiration for any underdog about to face a mighty team of stars.

Chance

There are different kinds of shock results. We usually think of individual games, such as Mexico beating Germany in the 2018 World Cup. There can be bigger surprises than that, however, since Mexico were a very good side prior to that match. A bigger World Cup shock was the USA beating England in the 1950 World Cup, which no one saw coming. The English FA Cup randomly sets entrants against each other and any team can enter as long as its ground has floodlights. Each season there are cases of lowly ranked teams beating better adversaries. In 1987 the competition threw up one of the biggest shocks possible when the FA Cup holders, Coventry City, were beaten by amateur side Sutton United.

More remarkable, however, are the surprise results we get of whole competitions, such as when Denmark (1992) and Greece (2004) became European champions. Of near-miraculous proportions was Leicester City's Premier League win of 2016. At the start of the season, they were favourites to be relegated and odds of 5,000–1 were being offered for them to be champions. The Premier League was seen as increasingly about the wealth of the clubs and it was becoming uncompetitive. The 'big six' were dominating, since they could afford to buy the top players and were scooping up all the TV and Champions League money. Leicester's triumph gave fresh hope to all other teams, in any level of any contest. It is a subjective judgement, but it was probably the most exciting Premier League season to that date. 'Neutral' supporters of other clubs got behind Leicester's efforts, with the few exceptions of their immediate rivals in the closing weeks of the campaign.

I can think of only one competition result that rivals Leicester's win for shock value, which was 'the Miracle of Bern': West Germany's first World Cup win in 1954. Outside of Germany, the passage of time has erased the extent of the surprise of this win. Germany had been reduced to rubble at the end of the war, just nine years before this tournament. In places, it still was little more than ruins and many Germans continued to struggle for basic nutrition. Reportedly, bookmakers were not even offering odds on West Germany winning the World Cup since they were clearly there just to make up the numbers. The world's best team, everyone agreed, were Hungary, who got through to the Final against the Germans with relative ease. Even at this stage, no one expected a German win since Hungary had beaten them 8–3 in the group stage 14 days earlier. A foregone conclusion? In the Final itself, Hungary took a 2–0 lead after eight minutes. What chance a

German victory at that point? That Germany won the game 3–2 is seen by many as the moment their post-war recovery really began. The team took the train back from Switzerland and when they crossed the border saw the new West German flag flying with pride for the first time since the end of the Nazi era. The revival in spirit became an industrial recovery. This is still the greatest story in the history of football. The reason for that, at least in part, is that it is also the greatest surprise.

Is unpredictability a flaw?

The sense that football seems particularly susceptible to surprise results has some statistical backing. In 2009, the *MIT Technology Review* reported on a statistical analysis that seemed to bear this out. Work by Gerald Skinner and Guy Freeman had aimed to find how often the best teams won. They discovered an alarmingly high number of inconsistent triplets. Where team A beats team B, and team B then beats team C, you would expect team A to beat team C. Of the games they considered between three such opponents, however, they found that 17% of such triplets were inconsistent. Here is a real such example. In the closing weeks of the Premier League campaign of 2017–18, Manchester United won 3–2 away at Manchester City. It was an important game because City would have won the title with a victory (and they were 2–0 up at half time). The following week, Manchester United, second in the league, were at home to bottom-placed West Bromwich Albion. Now, a few weeks before, West Bromwich had lost 3–0 at Manchester City. Without much experience of football, someone might reason that Manchester United beats Manchester City, Manchester City beats West Bromwich, therefore Manchester United beats West Bromwich. However, this became a conspicuous inconsistent triplet as Albion beat United 1–0 and City won the title without even playing that day. Skinner and Freeman report this as a flaw of the sport. If results occurred as a matter of pure chance, 25% of such triplets would exhibit the inconsistent feature described. If, in reality, 17% of triplets are inconsistent, it suggests that the outcomes in football are little better than chance. There has been other work by Scott Kretchmar in the *Journal of the Philosophy of Sport* pointing to similar 'game flaws', with some suggestions as to how they could be rectified to give the best teams a better chance of winning.

Such analyses, I believe, fail to grasp what sport is all about. A clue is to be found in the title of Skinner and Freeman's paper cited above, which is 'Soccer Matches as Experiments: How Often Does the "Best" Team Win?' Football matches are not experiments to see how often the best team wins, nor, contrary to Kretchmar's view, was a game flawed if the strongest team did not win. Sporting contests generally, and football matches in particular, are not just about determining which is the strongest side, nor should they be about arranging things to ensure that the stronger team can be guaranteed to triumph. Sport can give us so much more, including when it shows us that victory is sometimes possible against the odds. It seems plausible also that football would be not nearly so entertaining unless this were possible. Suppose the inconsistent triplets were 0% of the cases. Then when A has beaten B, and B has beaten C, what possible interest would A versus C be to anyone? Whether you support team A or C, it would be hard to get excited about it.

A further comparison with rugby is relevant here. In 1998 I was becoming a bit curious about Rugby League again. I was born in a rugby city that had no football team and I had seen a few rugby games but without ever being gripped. I noticed, however, that Dewsbury, a small-town, second-tier team, had drawn the mighty Wigan in the knockout Challenge Cup, so I went along out of curiosity.

Chance

Being a football fan, I had some hopes of seeing the smaller club put on a show and give their illustrious visitors a right good game. The hopes were dashed. Wigan ran out winners by 56–0. Within minutes, I could see that it was a no-contest and it quickly became one of the dullest sporting exhibitions I've seen. Among the eight other Fifth Round ties that weekend, there were results of 78–0, 6–48 and 84–6. The problem was that there were no giant-killings. A small difference in ability can translate into a huge difference in score in rugby, and that's boring. Because football is low scoring, and results can hinge on just a few key moments, everyone has a chance. Rugby League is a great sport with a rich sporting heritage, and the games between evenly balanced sides can be exciting. But it's just not football.

Out of control?

Unpredictable results are possible in football because players and coaches lack complete control over all that happens. A shot can hit the crossbar and fall down on the line. It could then, depending on the spin, bounce forward and over the line or backwards and out. The player taking the shot does not have mastery over determining which of these two outcomes occurs. It is doubtful that the striker was aiming to hit the crossbar in the first place, even though a player might aim for just inside the post or bar. No one would aim to score specifically via the bar and goal line, with forward spin taking the ball in, for such a shot would be impossible to execute reliably. Most likely, when this happens, the striker was aiming away from the goalkeeper but inside the goal and the shot was not precise enough to avoid it hitting the bar. The difference in outcome between these two possibilities, once the ball bounces on the line, is potentially huge and could certainly be game changing. When the ball bounces on the line and comes out, it could be caught by the keeper or cleared by a defender. When it goes in, it's as much a goal as any other. Outcomes can turn on these fine margins over which the players have little or no control, and in a low-scoring game such as football, it can be the difference between victory and defeat.

We should be clear what we mean by chance, since this plays such a crucial role in the unpredictability of outcomes. Let us say, then, that chance is where there are at least two possible, significantly different outcomes where no one has any substantial control over which of these outcomes occurs. Long passes, blocks and corner kicks all have an element of chance. A good player can play a long pass more accurately than a novice, but it is still only in a rough direction. Think, for example, of a player trying to land a ball on the centre spot from out wide on the wing. We would expect a professional to be able to get it fairly close but still with a margin of error of a few metres. The problem is that if the ball leaves the boot just a few degrees away from the intended angle of impact, over a 50-metre distance this can translate to missing the centre spot by a number of metres. Blocks and tackles can introduce a large element of chance, especially when they occur near to goal and result in the ball unexpectedly changing direction. In the 2018 World Cup group stages, we saw a number of goals scored in this chancy way. Diego Costa scored for Spain against Iran, for instance, when an attempted clearance was kicked against his knee and went in the bottom left of the goal in a direction the goalkeeper didn't foresee. Similarly, Sadio Mane scored for Senegal against Japan when the goalkeeper's low punch rebounded straight back off the striker's knee. Harry Kane scored his hat-trick goal against Panama without even knowing about it as a shot simply deflected off his heel when he was running across the 18-yard line. Paul Pogba was initially credited with a goal that turned out to be doubly lucky for France. As he was trying to control the ball, Australia's Aziz Behich attempted a clearance that unintentionally looped towards the goal. It then hit the crossbar but fell a centimetre or two over the goal line. None of these goals was under the control of their scorers. Neither Costa, Mane, nor Kane was even attempting shots and Behich was aiming to clear. Yet two of these goals were match-winners, and another contributed to a 2–2 draw. When a chance event, over which players have no substantial control, works out in your favour in a significant way, we say it is luck. When it works out against you, we call it bad luck.

There is plenty that the players cannot control. Consider a penalty kick. The penalty taker chooses whether to hit the ball left, right or down the middle. The kick scores only if the goalkeeper guesses wrong and doesn't get to it. Clearly the striker has little or no control over which way the goalkeeper dives (there might be *some* control since there are no rules against deceiving the keeper, such as looking one way and then shooting the other). Similarly, the goalkeeper makes a choice whether to dive left, right or remain upright. To save the kick, the ball has to be shot within a reachable direction and, similarly, the keeper has no control over where the kicker shoots. There is skill in both penalty taking and penalty goalkeeping. The taker should at least get it on target, for instance. But whether a goal is scored is an outcome over which no one can claim complete control.

There is no shortage of other instances of luck playing a role. There are blocks and ricochets in key areas, there are spinning balls that change direction unexpectedly, and there is sunlight that blinds the goalkeeper just as a shot is coming. Paul Peschisolido scored for Derby against Nottingham Forest in 2004 when the ball took an unexpected bounce off a plastic coffee cup that had blown on to the pitch just as the keeper was about to kick clear. Then, in 2009, Darren Bent scored an infamous deflected goal for Sunderland that went in off a supporter's beach ball that had strayed into the goal mouth, entirely deceiving Liverpool goalkeeper Pepe Reina. Final score: 1–0.

This last example raises another category that is beyond the players' control, namely the decisions of the referee. A player cannot control what the others do, but nor can they control the referee's choices. When Darren Bent's shot hit the beach ball, the referee should have stopped play and re-started with a drop-ball, since the beach ball was an outside interference. But this is a rare incident in football and the referee made a mistake. The 2018 World Cup was the first in which use was made of VAR (video assistant referee) technology, which minimized the chance of certain types of refereeing mistakes. But it was used only for certain categories of decision, namely penalty awards and red card offences. The rest was still at the discretion of the referee. And even some of the penalties remained debated. VAR was indecisive in the awards of Iran's penalty against Portugal and France's against Croatia in the Final, since judgement and interpretation are still required. There will be borderline cases that remain indeterminate, no matter how many times they are seen, so opinions cannot be eradicated from the game. It has to be pointed out too that it is only the elite level of the game that can afford VAR and goal-line technology. Most football matches are dependent upon technologically unassisted decisions, which are crucial not just for penalty awards but also for offside calls, where goals can be scored or chalked off.

It is clear that there are simply too many variables for any player, spectator or pundit to calculate and reliably predict the outcome of some particular incident or final score in advance. Even if football were a game of simple geometrical calculation, a bit like snooker, and all physical movements of the ball and players were entirely deterministic matters, so much of what happens in the game is down to individual choices of the players, coaches and officials. There is as yet no remotely plausible account of the mind in physically deterministic terms that would allow a physicist to predict individuals' decisions. We have to assume that no one has full control over what happens in football.

What's the advantage in being the best?

Skinner and Freeman were right that football is full of chance. But it is not entirely full. If results were entirely predictable, there would be little interest in them. But if results were entirely unpredictable, that would be no better. Coin tossing would make a poor spectator sport, as would any other game of pure chance. We don't need that the best team always wins, but we want at least that the best teams will tend to win, otherwise it would not be a proper sporting contest of skill and effort. It would not be a contest at all.

We must insist that being the best team cannot be determined solely by whether that team wins the game or not. This would make 'being the best team' explanatorily redundant, since it would be only true by definition that the best team was the one that won. We call this a trivial explanation: A was better than B since A beat B and beating a team is what it means to be better than them. The problem with treating the matter as trivial, in this way, is that being a better side should be a possible explanation of why a weaker side was beaten and such an explanation cannot be merely in terms of a definition.

Victories are explicable in terms of one side having better skill, strength, speed and tactics than the other. These things – let us call them the sporting excellences of football – provide game advantages to the better team. We could interpret a game of football as a contest between the two sides' relative sporting excellences. These excellences will be specific to football. They are the athletic virtues that tend towards success. Height is an essential advantage in basketball but not always in football, since some roles are best filled by players with a low centre of gravity. And speed is an advantage in football but not in weightlifting.

Nevertheless, I am very deliberately saying only that the sporting excellences 'tend' to success. What exactly a tendency means is something that is often misunderstood, both in sport and in philosophy. A tendency is no guarantee of something happening. There is a tendency if there is a better than pure chance possibility of it happening, though. Thus, it is true that struck matches tend to light. It is perfectly possible to strike a match and it doesn't light: for instance, if there is a gust of wind at the time. But struck matches often do light, whereas they have no tendency to evaporate or dissolve. Similarly, a team with relatively greater football-related sporting excellence than another will tend to beat that side. There is no guarantee that they will, since the weaker side might get lucky, in some way, or they might manifest their excellences better during the 90 minutes of play. It is one thing to have a skill, for instance, but another thing to manifest it. Lionel Messi is considered one of the most skilful players in the current game, but when Argentina lost miserably 3–0 to Croatia in the 2018 World Cup, he never really manifested any of it. Messi was one of the top five players in the world, but ineffective in this instance. Why it's easy to manifest skills in one game and not in another is something the coaches of players will ponder, but one obvious answer is opportunity. A striker might have an expert skill at scoring free kicks from 25 metres. A good defensive option is to give no such free kicks away.

There is no necessity in the strongest team winning, therefore, but a tendency means more than that it has the mere possibility of winning. If the same two teams played each other over and over again, it would be rational to expect the best team to win more times than the weaker team (again, we will avoid treating this trivially, as true by definition). In a one-off encounter, however, such as a knock-out cup competition, the weaker team has a chance and can produce a surprise result. A full league season thus seems 'fairer' in the sense that there are enough sporting encounters for the stronger team's tendency to win, to display itself. A weak team might fluke one win, but it is unlikely to fluke 38 of them. Whether you prefer to see league matches or knock-out games is up to you.

The optimum balance

The Otago philosopher David Ward once said to me that a good sport would have the optimum balance between skill and luck. I think that football has it. There are too many factors for anyone to control to ensure that skill will always win the day. If it did, it would be boring to see that the stronger team always prevailed. It is a mistake to think that the alternative to this is pure chance, however. That would be just as boring to watch. There is plenty of luck in football, but it is not all luck. The fact that 17% of triplets are inconsistent is not a game flaw. Instead it can be considered as just one quantitative marker of the balance between skill and luck in football. If that figure were 25%, the game would be all luck and no skill. If it were 0%, the game would be all skill and no luck. The fact that football is the world's most popular spectator sport tells us that a figure of 17% might be just about right: the most interesting, the most entertaining, the optimum balance.

That we want such a balance is revealing. Either to play or watch, we want sports in which everyone has a chance. Why bother playing if you have no chance? Why bother training and practising if it does not increase your likelihood of victory? Sport is for both the winners and the losers. Both have to get something from it. It has to be worth all the effort. This can only be explained if we accept that the better teams have a tendency – but no more than a tendency – to win. Tendencies can come in degrees, of course. The 2018 Manchester City side will have had a much stronger tendency to beat Accrington Stanley, for instance, than they will have had to beat Arsenal. You would not rate Accrington's chances very highly, even in a one-off contest, but it is still worth it for them to turn up and give it their best shot. This is the key to sporting contests. It is what makes sport a contest.

It is hard not to draw parallels between football and regular, non-sporting life. You cannot control everything that happens to you, or guarantee that you will get the rewards that you deserve. There is a flip-side to that, however, for which football can provide the lesson. Even if you find yourself in an adverse situation, where the odds are stacked against your success, you see that your best efforts might still get you through. This doesn't mean that if you fail, it was because you did not try hard enough. Football teams often give their very best and lose. In football as in life, however, your best efforts can still come up short.

6

Victory

Football stories

It is all too easy to remember the victories and forget the defeats. Victory is the aim and the glory. Defeat is painful. Would it be any wonder if we had a selective memory bias towards victory and found it better to set aside defeat to some dark, neglected corner of the mind?

I don't think I am alone in having a selective memory, given what I hear from other fans. They all talk about their past glories. Liverpool fans reminisce about the 'Miracle of Istanbul' 2005 Champions League success, England supporters still talk of the spirit of 1966, and every time I've visited Oxford United there's always some reference in the programme to their Milk Cup triumph of 1986. Liverpool fans won't talk so much about the 2018

Champions League defeat in the coming years, the seasons they crashed out earlier in the competition, or the time they blew the Premier League title from a winning position in 2014, even though they had Luis Suárez in the team. England fans have to remember 1966 since it's the only competition the national team have won and the story since has been one of failure. And it's understandable that Oxford United remind their success-deprived fans that they did once win a national trophy since they need to give them some hope.

Stories matter to us; and a football club with a long history will have many of them. Stories do not just exist on their own, independently of our thoughts and wishes. We create them, and the same set of bare facts can generate any number of very different tales. A narrative can be woven from the basic material that football results provide. The cliché is for stories in sport to end with victory. Consider how many films about sport conclude with the final win, and then the closing credits roll. Such a narrative can be constructed for just about any team. Sheffield United have a recent history of failure, for example, but I can still tell you how six seasons in the third tier finally resolved when former player Chris Wilder took over as coach in 2016, got the team playing proper football with attacking flair, and took the division by storm. The reality is, however, that there are no end credits to be rolled in football. There is always another game to be played and another season ahead. The lift that a win gives to the fans might last only a few days until the next match, when defeat is risked once more. Still, it's the win that will be remembered and the defeat forgotten.

As with all matters that we view through a philosophical lens, though, when we look deeper we see that the relationship between fans and victory is more complex than the above account pretends. There is seldom an absolute rule in philosophical theories. There are, after all, occasions when fans enjoy a tale of tragic defeat. This does not mean that those fans enjoy the defeats, of course, but loss can feed into a narrative with which fans identify and take some pleasure in recounting. There can be one-off instances of monumental defeats that feed into a particular outlook of shared suffering, such as when Brazil's 1950 World Cup loss became part of the national psyche. There are also stories of heroic defeats, especially from underdog teams who push a bigger opponent hard but then lose at the last moment. Honour can be maintained in such circumstances.

What I mainly have in mind, though, are those

fans who are content to describe themselves as long-suffering, who think there is something heroic in a love that endures despite a lack of success. They can regard themselves as genuine fans, as opposed to the 'glory hunters'. It can be dismissed as easy to support a team like Manchester United, Chelsea or Real Madrid since that is almost always about winning. Those supporters don't know what true love for a team is, however, since they have never really had their resolve tested. There are clubs that are a lot less successful than Sheffield United, but even we talk about all the losing cup semi-finals we have experienced in recent years, along with eight attempts at promotion through the play-offs, all of which failed. There is indeed something noble in defeat. Anthony Skillen once wrote a paper called 'Sport is for Losers'. It really is: consider the World Cup finals, where of the 32 teams that start out, 31 of them go home as losers, and that's not to mention all those that don't even reach the finals. Football can be the ideal testing ground for learning to lose. Life is full of defeats from which you have to recover and fight another day. Sport provides a harmless arena for coping with such set-backs, since nothing really hinges on the results. Disappointment is the norm to all but a few in football, but what an education that experience can provide.

Victory

The dynamic

We can still make a good story, then, and learn some lessons from defeat. But there is no instance in which defeat is ever the aim in football, unless the game is fixed in some way. Everyone wants to win, and that provides what I call the dynamic of football.

There is a distinction to be drawn, however, between wanting to win and aiming to win. Victory is the dynamic in football because of the former but not necessarily the latter. The distinction is required because there are clear cases in football where a team is aiming not to win but to do something else. As we get to the end of a league campaign, for example, there comes a point where some teams can no longer, not even mathematically, win the championship. They may still aim to win individual games, but this is not because they seek to win the league, since they know they cannot. Rather, they will have more modest ambitions, such as to finish as high as possible in the league or simply to avoid relegation. There can be financial incentives behind these aims, but even if not, pride still counts for a lot, as does a desire to do as well as one possibly can. The latter is a big factor in sport. In the London marathon, for example, there are thousands of entrants but only one winner. The vast majority know they have virtually no chance of winning. But that is not their aim. Instead, they might want to beat their personal best time or, if it's a debut marathon, just to complete it at all. People take pleasure in maximizing their potential, and this seems to apply just as much to professional sportsmen and -women. Some might have an unrealistic over-estimation of what their potential is, and have harsh lessons to learn. In other instances, though, there seems nothing so tragic in sport as when someone fails to realize their potential, because of either bad luck or personal failings. In such a context, it is perfectly reasonable for some teams and players to be satisfied with relatively modest ambitions, such as avoiding relegation.

This means, too, that there might be individual games in which they are not aiming to win. They might hope to win but also know that avoidance of defeat is enough to finish above the relegation zone. Footballers always say that it is hard to play for a draw, but there are plenty of matches in which teams behave as if they are at least content with such an outcome. Take the France–Denmark game in the 2018 World Cup. The French knew that a draw was enough to win the group while the Danes knew, once they heard the score in the other group game, that a draw would see them through to the next stage. Either team would have taken a goal if it came their way but, since both were happy to avoid defeat, a 0–0 result was the natural consequence. I also see nothing wrong in another kind of case, where a team realizes that it's in for a beating and reduces its aim merely to keeping the score down. This could count for goal difference, in some competitions, but there is also the matter of pride where a 5–0 defeat looks considerably worse than a 2–0 defeat.

There are perfectly understandable instances, therefore, when victory is not the aim. But it remains the dynamic, I say, since it is what each team wants, hopes for and does what it can to maximize the chances of getting. Avoiding relegation makes sense if you have hopes that next season you could win, and since this is exactly what happened to Leicester City in 2015–16, the hope seems valid.

Victory is the dynamic in the sense that it is the incentive. There is little other incentive that the game can offer, after all. It is what drives teams on to further effort, straining to the last in order to achieve it. It is what directs their overall endeavour. It is what coaches are ultimately judged on: perhaps not always the *final* victory, but at least how many victories are achieved during the campaign.

Victory is the dynamic in that it is what counts as success in the game. Playing the most beautiful football, in contrast, does not count as success if it is accompanied by defeat. A team that consistently 'achieved' beautiful defeats would be rightly criticized as failures. Victory accompanied by beauty might be praised, but the praise follows because the team is victorious. Beautiful football gains a team additional credit if it is also successful, but beauty without success gets little credit. Defeated coaches even feel patronized if opposing coaches praise their style of play. Any coach would prefer to win ugly than to lose beautifully.

Victory is the dynamic in that it explains what the players do when they are playing football. Suppose you received an alien visitor who really knew nothing at all about football and you took them to a game. This theoretical visitor might ask why a player passes the ball, why the players are running so hard, why they kick or trip each other, and so on. You might be able to explain these actions in terms of something else: the players want to stop their opponents, they want to get into a good scoring position, and so on. But the visitor could well ask why they want to do those things as well. Eventually, you might just have to say that the players are performing those actions ultimately because they want to win. If you are asked why they want to win, there seems no further, informative answer. They just do. That's the point. If they didn't want to win, in a sense they wouldn't properly be playing at all. And if you wanted to know why people like winning things, the answer would be found not in football itself, but most likely in psychology, philosophy or sociology, some might even say evolutionary biology. Apart from that, all that we can say about a football match is that the players are performing the actions they do because they believe that in some way those actions will, in the circumstances, contribute towards increasing the chances of victory. Footballers often fail, of course. They make mistakes when they lack skill or are beginning to tire, late in the game. But they will always try the best they can to make a positive contribution to success even if they cannot always execute their plans.

Victory is the dynamic, too, of the excitement of football. The main things that excite fans are the moments that contribute most to the chance of victory: getting the ball in the opponent's goal mouth, a wing-back beating a defender, a ball being cleared off one's own line and, ultimately, the scoring of goals. The most exciting moment of all is that winner in the closing minutes, where there is almost no time for the opposition to reply. The game changes, at the last opportunity, from uncertainty to a likely win. The goal scoring is even more exciting than the blowing of the final whistle, at which point the victory becomes definite. The excitement is in the changing of the game, imposing on it a new outlook, more so than the official ending of the game. When a team has a single-goal lead, it is relief that accompanies the game's end. It is not so much that a victory has occurred that creates the excitement but that a victory is in the process of being achieved.

Competition

This talk of winning brings into question competitiveness itself. Some people are not competitive at all. Football is most likely not for them. Winning is of no interest to them, they might say. Someone like this might enjoy sport and physical activity but prefer to do yoga or go jogging. These are uncompetitive sports. It is hard to argue against someone who adopts this attitude. One reason might be that they simply hate losing and perhaps think that the joy of winning does not compensate for the pain of defeat. It might be that they are actually competitive after all: competitive people really hate losing, so much so that they would rather not compete in the first place.

Another way in which someone can be uncompetitive is that they really don't see the point of competition, or think that it is not fair, or that it is not the right way for people to behave. After all, someone wins only if someone else loses and is then unhappy. Is it right to enjoy winning if you know you have saddened someone else? Isn't that selfish? In other walks of life, we like to cooperate and do things together, finding solutions from which all benefit. The neoliberal political agenda has introduced competition into areas of society that many think inappropriate, such as universities, railways and hospitals. Shouldn't we resist this ruthless, selfish agenda?

There is no answer to someone who simply sees no point in winning. However, it need not follow that being non-competitive, when it comes to resourcing the health service, requires a parallel rejection of competitive sports. Instead, it might be that there are some practices where competition is appropriate and others where it's not. Sport is mainly harmless, since, as I've said, nothing significant hinges on it. It is a 'safe' space in which to find competition fun, since the losers should not be materially damaged.

I can have fun watching Sheffield United since when they lose it does not lower my salary, make me ill or increase the chance of world war. If football did any of those things, we would need to look again. In the health service, people's lives can, indeed, be at stake. There would then need to be good evidence that competition was not risking harm.

It would, in any case, be an over-simplification to think that football is solely about competition. As explained in detail in chapter 3, football is primarily a team sport and, to that extent, any competitive success is also founded on cooperation and togetherness. Victory provides the unity of purpose that can bring together 11 individuals and see them merge into an organic whole. A team in which the players saw each other as rivals – for adulation, fame, the highest salary or just a place in the starting line-up – would be unlikely to maximize its potential. Rather, it tends to success in football if the players can put the interests of the team ahead of their personal ones. It is no real surprise, then, that football is conducive also to a socialist interpretation. Socrates – the Brazilian footballer rather than the Greek philosopher – famously championed this leftist vision of the game. It can be felt also among the fans who find their own identities sometimes subsumed into that of the crowd, united by a shared purpose, love and loyalty. There is, thus, a tension and a balancing between competitive and cooperative strands in football, as in a number of other team sports. It is through cooperation that the chances of competitive success will be highest.

The paradox

That victory determines the dynamic of football is a claim that has a bearing on a topic that we considered earlier and to which we can now return in a better position to understand. In chapter 2, we noted that football produces aesthetic value. Some speak of this in terms of beauty, but we saw that there are distinct and specific aesthetic categories that apply to football. We also saw, however, that a chip shot is more aesthetically appealing when it scores a goal than when it misses. We can now explain why, with reference to victory. We have also noted that victory is not exactly the aim of playing football, since there are some instances where one can play without aiming to win, but that football does nevertheless have a close connection with the desire for victory. I said that victory provides football's dynamic, by which I mean that it explains what happens on the football field and can be taken as the end in itself when playing, since there is nothing further that can be desired by someone playing or watching it.

The analysis puts us in a position to resolve a dispute between *futebol arte*, embodied by the Brazil team of 1970, and the artless *futebol de resultados* taken to extremes by Argentina's Estudiantes in the 1960s, and a number of others. Is football about creating art or getting results? On the basis of what has gone before, we come down on the side of results. Victory is what we want. As before, though, this verdict has to be qualified, and when we look at the nuances we find a surprising, almost paradoxical, result.

The aim of football is not to create art. Were any player to have such an aim, it is arguable that they would no longer be playing football at all but be engaged in some other activity. I had a frustrating personal experience that shows this. In 2002 I went to see Paris St Germain play the Hungarian side Újpest in the UEFA Cup. Ronaldinho scored an early goal and there was soon another from Pochettinho, giving PSG a comfortable lead. The two-legged tie was far from over, however. With the away leg to come, Ronaldinho nevertheless decided to put on a show of tricks and ball-juggling during the game. Some in the crowd were happy, but I wasn't. I didn't see that any of his actions increased the chance of PSG scoring, which they should have tried to do with the tie still alive. The problem I had was that if he was trying to display artistry, to literally be an artist, then his primary purpose was no longer to win. He had effectively ceased playing football. Now ball-juggling can be impressive to watch, since it requires a high level of skill and coordination. But it is a skill that has only minimal relevance to a game of football. Good ball control might help beat a defender, but no one needs keepie-uppie to do that. Because Ronaldinho's play did not contribute to the prospects of the team, I should add that I found it neither beautiful nor entertaining. I was there to see football. There seems to be a consequence, therefore, that if your aim is to create beauty, then you cease to play football. As a result, even if you do produce beauty, it is not beautiful football, since it is not any kind of football. This is the first side of what I call the paradox.

The second side is this. It is in striving for victory that the aesthetic values of the game are realized. Wanting to win is what makes the player run as fast as they can, displaying a fluid, efficient motion, being quick, dashing, dynamic. The desire to score is what makes a striker leap as high as possible, looking to get a header in on goal, emerging from a cluster of surrounding defenders. The urgent need to stop a goal-bound shot is what makes the goalkeeper dive and attain full extension of their body, almost as if they can fly. We witness the human form pushed to its limits. Any player who doesn't really want to win, in contrast, is likely to not push themselves, not run in the strongest way they can, not strain every muscle to get as high as they can, and not make every effort to curl in a shot from 25 metres.

Similarly, we see sporting drama in the quest for victory. That Liverpudlian miracle in Istanbul would not have happened without the incentive of victory. Why try to pull back a 3–0 deficit otherwise? Some of the greatest games are those where the lead changes hands, when we move from 1–2, to 3–2, to 3–4. It is in the desperate effort to win that this dramatic beauty is really produced. When teams do not have an incredibly strong desire to win, as neither France nor Denmark did in that 2018 World Cup game, we get very little to please the eye. Both sides were booed off the pitch. Our inevitable conclusion, then, is that beauty is produced in football when it is not the aim. It is instead when the team wants to win that it creates aesthetic value in its play.

We can now sum up the paradox thus: if you aim for beauty in football, then you will not get it. If you aim instead to win, then that is when you might create beauty. This sounds puzzling, as paradoxes do, but we can now understand the message behind it: if you want beauty, then you should play to win. This conclusion also explains why it is the successful shots, crosses, dribbles, passing moves and free-kick routines that are the most beautiful. If you just watch the flight of the ball, a shot that misses by a couple of centimetres is superficially not all that different from one that goes an inch the other side of the post and in. There can be a significant aesthetic difference between the successful shot and the unsuccessful one, however, since the former contributes to the win. We might see countless slow-motion replays of the scoring shot, but only a single replay of the miss.

Now it might be pointed out that what I have offered is not strictly a paradox, as understood by a philosopher of logic, for instance. A paradox is where apparently valid reasoning from apparently true premises produces a false or self-contradictory conclusion. What I have presented is a paradox in the less formal sense, however, where what would usually be regarded as standard reasoning is rejected as false. My account of aesthetics and the aims of football is similar to the so-called paradox of happiness (see chapter 7 of Mike Martin's *Happiness and the Good Life*). If you want to be happy, you won't get it by pursuing happiness. You have to do other things, and then happiness might come to you indirectly. The air of paradox in both this and my account is that they say that if you want something, P, then aim at something other than P, and then you might get P. In the cases of both happiness and aesthetics in football, it is plausible that this unexpected structure is exhibited.

Perhaps I am overlooking something significant in my account of the desire to win. Am I not romanticizing football in claiming that the desire to win is what produces football's beauty? The philosophy of win at all costs also produces what is ugly in football. It gives us dirty fouls, play acting, time-wasting, brute force. It gave us the long-ball game. It gave us Maradona's 'hand of god'. It has sometimes given us racist abuse, biting and the use of performance-enhancing drugs. None of that was pretty. This only supports the claim that football is about victory, primarily, and any subsequent beauty is a by-product of that quest. The beautiful moments of football might be rare, but it is not surprising that they get a disproportionately large share of the attention. Aesthetic experiences are precious and worth waiting for. I often look at countless paintings in the art gallery before finding one that really moves me. Why should football be any different? As with art, it is the greatest works that will be remembered. Teams that win ugly, playing football the wrong way, will find that they do not endure in the fans' hearts. Football is capable of far more than that.

I have explained during this book that there are good reasons why the game of football can mean so much to so many people. Initially, it has a superficial appeal, and this might attract its younger enthusiasts. It is an allure based around excitement, colour and glory. Football would not have the popularity it enjoys if it were only that, however, for it can also attract a more sophisticated and thoughtful viewer. The game has an intellectual depth that rewards more detailed consideration, and I have outlined just some of the ideas to be found in it: that teams are interacting wholes, capable of changing the individuals that make them up; that the sport balances a set of athletic virtues against chance elements in a seemingly optimal way; that aesthetic appeal can be found where victory is the aim; and that success can be dependent on the control and exploitation of space. The best coaches understand the philosophical richness of football probably as well as anyone, for it is they who have to solve the myriad problems in the way of their victories. But we outside observers can have the pleasure of understanding these footballing solutions too. My hope is that a reader who has come this far will be looking at their next game even more closely than usual and thinking their own thoughts about the nature of this wondrous creation of the human spirit. I have covered a select few topics, but the contemplative inspiration that football offers seems inexhaustible.

References and
Further Reading

Brown, P., *Savage Enthusiasm: A History of Football Fans*, County Durham: Goal Post, 2017.

Critchley, S., *What We Think About When We Think About Football*, London: Profile, 2017.

de Sousa, R., *The Rationality of Emotion*, Cambridge, MA: MIT Press, 1987.

Hornby, N., *Fever Pitch*, London: Gollancz, 1992.

Hunt, C., *World Cup Stories*, Ware, Herts: Interact, 2006.

Kretchmar, R.S., 'Game Flaws', *Journal of the Philosophy of Sport*, vol. 32, no. 1 (2005), pp. 36–48.

Martin, M.W, *Happiness and the Good Life*, Oxford: Oxford University Press, 2012.

MIT Technology Review, 'The Statistical Problem with Soccer', 29 September 2009, *https://www.technolo gyreview.com/s/415507/the-statistical-problem-with-soccer/*.

Mumford, S., *Watching Sport: Aesthetics, Ethics and Emotions*, London: Routledge, 2011.

Papineau, D., *Knowing the Score: How Sport Teaches Us About Philosophy (and Philosophy About Sport)*, London: Constable, 2017.

Reid, H., *Introduction to the Philosophy of Sport*, Lanham, MD: Rowman & Littlefield, 2012.

Russell, B., *In Praise of Idleness and Other Essays*, London: Routledge, 2004.

Ryall, E., *Philosophy of Sport: Key Questions*, London: Bloomsbury, 2016.

Skillen, A., 'Sport is for Losers', in M.J. McNamee and S.J. Parry (eds), *Ethics and Sport*, London: E & FN Spon, 1998, pp. 169–81.

Skinner, G. and G. Freeman, 'Soccer Matches as Experiments: How Often Does the "Best" Team Win?' *Journal of Applied Statistics*, vol. 36, no. 10 (2009), pp. 1087–95.

Suits, B., *The Grasshopper: Games, Life and Utopia*, 2nd edn, Peterborough, Ont.: Broadview Press, 2005.

Wilson, J., *Inverting the Pyramid*, 2nd edn, London: Orion, 2013.